WHAT YOU DIDN'T KNOW IS HOLDING
YOU BACK IN **BUSINESS**

SHE
RULES

SARA ROACH LEWIS

SHE RULES: WHAT YOU DIDN'T KNOW IS HOLDING YOU BACK IN BUSINESS

Published by **SRL Solutions**
St. Peters Bay, PEI

ISBN: 978-1-7779036-0-2

BUS109000   BUSINESS & ECONOMICS / Women in Business

Cover, Interior design and Illustrations by Lorie Miller Hansen
Technical Build by Andrea Cinnamond

QUANTITY PURCHASES: Schools, companies, professional groups, clubs, and other organizations may qualify for special terms when ordering quantities of this title. For information, email info@sherules.biz.

Printed in Canada.

WWW.**SHERULES**.BIZ

I would like to acknowledge that this book was written in Mi'kma'ki, the traditional and unceeded territory of the Mi'kmaq. I pay respect to the Indigenous Mi'kmaq People, past, present and future, who have occupied this Island for over 12,000 years.

Our name, Epekwitk, roughly translates to "cradled on water". I recognize and honor the Mi'kmaq for our respective rights to reside here in harmony and for the continued wellbeing of this territory.

I strive to work together with the Mi'kmaq and other Indigenous nations to preserve the lands and waters and to live out our roles and responsibilities as a settler within the sacred Treaties of Peace and Friendship.

Mi'kma'ki is the word for the Mi'kmaq Traditional territory including all of Prince Edward Island & Nova Scotia, eastern New Brunswick, Gaspé Peninsula, & southern Newfoundland.

TO SUSAN
How blessed are we to have
a lifelong friendship where our paths
have intertwined, diverged, and weaved
together so beautifully?

...and **TO SCOTT**
For keeping me grounded and fully
supporting my dreams.

"*There are oppressive, patriarchal systems in place.* **Systems designed to keep you overworking and under-earning.**

Systems that have existed for centuries, designed to keep **women and people of colour struggling and broke.**"

Rachel Rodgers. Author, **We should all be millionaires**

"*Our deepest fear is not that we are inadequate.* **Our deepest fear is that we are powerful beyond measure. It is our light, not our darkness that most frightens us.** *We ask ourselves, 'Who am I to be brilliant, gorgeous, talented, fabulous?'*

Actually, who are you not to be? You are a child of God. Your playing small does not serve the world. *There is nothing enlightened about shrinking so that other people won't feel insecure around you.* **We are all meant to shine, as children do.**"

Marianne Williamson, **A Return to Love: Reflections on the Principles of "A Course in Miracles"**

CONTENTS

CONTENTS CONTINUED...

CONTENTS CONTINUED...

PREFACE

How do women succeed in a world where the rules of business were inspired by war strategy and written by men?
Answer: We make our own rules.

You started your business for freedom and flexibility and yet, here you are, often overwhelmed and feeling like a hamster stuck on a wheel. You're working hard and grinding it out—squeezing in family and life responsibilities and occasionally remembering to take care of yourself. Feeling guilty for the balls that get dropped. Beating yourself up for not doing enough, no matter how hard you work.

Can I let you in on a secret? It's not your fault. It's nothing you've done wrong. It's simply that the traditional rules of business don't apply that well to you. Which is why we're changing them.

This book will help you rewrite your rules for business. She Rules will leave you feeling inspired, validated, comforted, and re-motivated. You'll have a greater understanding of how being a woman impacts your experience in business and how you can use that to your benefit to feel more confident, be in control, and make more money.

That weight you feel on your shoulders (or on your chest or in your belly) will ease because you'll learn that what you're feeling is not all about you. You'll learn how to shed your imposter syndrome and relax into your zone of genius so that even when you're going all in, it won't feel like you're working hard.

This is not a "get rich quick" book. It won't give you strategies on how to "skip the grind," but it will reveal secrets to help you grow your business to where you actually have the flexibility and freedom you crave.

Why am I so confident? Because as an expert in gender equity, I understand what makes you tick. I've made a career out of supporting women as they shed society's expectations of them, break the rules when necessary, and create new pathways for success. All while working to change the systems that don't work for women's lives.

I come from an entrepreneurial family in a tiny rural town, which taught me to value community and competition.

As a business owner, I live with wild ambition and a desire for more. More wealth, more freedom, more time, more fun. And as a feminist business strategist, I've helped clients overcome huge challenges and hit massive revenue targets.

I want more for all women because I have a vision for this world we live in. One that is more equitable and just. One where women's voices are honoured, valued, and amplified. One where women make lots of their own damn money, solving their own damn problems.

So, dig in for the small tweaks and the profound shifts She Rules will bring to you. Skip around. Take breaks. Write in the margins. Embrace what speaks to you. Leave the rest.

SETTING THE STAGE

I am on a mission to increase the number of women who have million-dollar businesses.

You may be surprised to know that my mission is informed by a lifetime of working toward issues of social justice. I spent many years leading a feminist organization, where my friend and colleague Michelle and I secured more than $8 million dollars in project funding. I got to work with hundreds of women from all walks of life on dozens of projects and initiatives.

One of those projects was called "Paths to Prosperity: A Community Response to Poverty." I led a team that included researchers from the local university, organizational staff, and a dozen subject matter experts —women living in poverty . . . women experiencing the weight of broken systems.

How inspiring it was to see some of our subject matter experts build their confidence, make new community connections, and overcome their nerves to present our report with its suite of recommendations to community leaders, including the premier and caucus.

It was both difficult and amazing to delve deeply into poverty—the swirly mess of data, stories, cause and effect, intergenerational impacts, stigma, inequality... So complicated and challenging and yet, so simple—don't we all want to live in a world where everyone has their needs met? And don't we have enough abundance to make that happen?

In part, Paths to Prosperity inspired my new career as a business coach for women. Life is hard. And it's really freaking hard when you live in poverty. Money doesn't buy happiness, but it does have a positive impact on your health and well-being. If you want to change the world, empower women to solve problems and make more money. Because when women have more money, they share the wealth with their children, their families, and their community.

Deeply understanding that poverty is at the root of many of the challenges women face in their life, I chose to focus on supporting women to create their own *economic prosperity,* as we say in the report-writing speak of my old world. Business strategy feeds me in a lot of ways, and knowing that it helps women improve their financial wealth is a biggie.

Even though I spent much of my adult life addressing the inequality that women face in life, I didn't expect to see so much of it in the business world.

Wow, was I wrong.

Early in my new career, I worked with Invest Ottawa, an economic development organization that works to build a strong technology-focused business ecosystem. I was hired to help create gender, equity, and inclusion guidelines for the organization. They were interested in focusing on supporting more women in all areas of their organization.

In Canada, 37% of self-employed people are women, and just over 15% of businesses with at least one employee are women-owned (Women Entrepreneurship Knowledge Hub, 2020). While this is encouraging, women-owned businesses are less likely to be considered high growth, which means having more than a 20% increase in revenues over three years (Women Entrepreneurship Knowledge Hub, 2020).

In 2017, the McKinsey Report presented an even bleaker picture, reporting that at this rate of progress, it will take 180 years for women to reach parity in entrepreneurship (Devillard et al., 2019).

UGH.

Make no mistake: There are trailblazing women in business. Women have been running laundry stands, restaurants, brothels, daycares, and alehouses since the beginning of time. And they've been behind the scenes in their family businesses, shouldering much of the work and little of the glory.

At the beginning of the 1900s, there were women like Madam CJ Walker, the first self-made Black woman millionaire (Bundles, 2020). She became a millionaire by solving a problem she knew and understood—finding good hair and beauty products for Black women. She's an inspiration, not only because of her business savvy, but also because she also became a philanthropist and a political and social activist. She used her money to make the change she wanted to see in the world.

Often, women found themselves in business out of necessity, like Janet Johnston, who ran Johnston's Lobster Factory here on Prince Edward Island in the late 1930s and 1940s. She picked up her husband's duties when he died suddenly. While I'm sure she faced significant challenges, she is remembered as well loved and respected in the community as an employer and fish buyer (Johnston, 1983).

Despite stories of amazing women entrepreneurs who overcame incredible challenges, women-owned businesses are still a relatively new phenomenon. We often forget this because women have discovered entrepreneurship and embraced it—the number of women entrepreneurs has almost quadrupled over the last 40 years, growing at almost three times the rate of men entrepreneurs (Bouchard & Bédard-Maltais, 2019).

But it's not without challenges.

We couldn't get a bank account on our own in Canada until 1964—a full decade later in the US (PSAC, 2019). Weirder than that, it wasn't until 1988 that the US Congress passed the Women's Business Ownership Act, eliminating outdated laws that required a husband's signature on business documents, including getting a bank loan (Women's Business Ownership Act, 1988). Let that sink in for a moment. The actual structures wouldn't allow us to start a business without hubby's permission until I was sixteen years old. In 1988 … when I was dreaming about being Melanie Griffin in *Working Girl* with her boxy blazer and office of her own.

But Sara, you're thinking, *this is not the world anymore.*

Actually, it is. Women:

- Shoulder more responsibility for household chores, regardless of whether they work outside the home or if there are children in the home—to the tune of an extra five hours of work per day (Hayes et al., 2020).

- Spend more time with their kids than housewives did in the 60s (Dotti Sani & Treas, 2016).

- Are underrepresented in all positions of power and leadership, where decisions are made that affect people's lives: corporate, government, public service, and education (Catalyst, 2020; UN Women, 2021; Shi et al., 2019; Whitford, 2020).

- Are portrayed in the media with unrealistic body expectations, speak half as much as men do on screen, and represent only 13% of subjects and sources in the television newscasts monitored (Allen, 2018; Geena Davis Inclusion Quotient; Global Media Monitoring Project, 2021).

- Experience violence, harassment, and sexual assault at significantly greater levels than men (Government of Canada, 2021).

- At all levels, earn just 76.8 cents for every dollar that men earn (Canadian Women's Foundation, 2021).

- Earn/pay themselves 28% less than men entrepreneurs (Freshbooks, 2018).

- Receive less than 3% of all Venture Capital Funding (Bittner & Lau, 2021).

- Face barriers accessing loans and capital for their business ventures (Taylor, 2019).

The gap is even wider for Black, Indigenous women of colour, women with disabilities, and 2SLGBTQ+ people. In fact:

- Indigenous women working full time, full year earn an average of 35% less than non-Indigenous men, earning 65 cents to the dollar. (Canadian Women's Foundation, 2021).

- Racialized women working full time, full year earn an average of 33% less than non-racialized men, earning 67 cents to the dollar. (Canadian Women's Foundation, 2021).

- Newcomer women working full time, full year earn an average of 29% less than non-newcomer men, earning 71 cents to the dollar. (Canadian Women's Foundation, 2021).

I don't tell you this to depress you. This is simply the reality. And it ain't pretty. Things are clearly not working in our favour.

By the way, if you need to take a little break from the weight you may feel from reading those statistics, then feel free to wander off. Rage a bit, shake your head in disbelief, be pissed off. But do come back because there are solutions.

So, what's a gal to do? We want flexibility. And freedom. We want to serve our clients. And make positive changes in the world. We want to create meaningful employment for others. We want to create a legacy. We want to make money. We want the scale to tip in our favour sometimes or at least not have it weighted against us.

We've got the evidence (like it or not) that the business world is not an even playing field (see above). To better understand why, it's important to understand that traditional business strategy is based on a male-dominated military strategy. *The Art of War* by Sun Tzu, written in 500 BCE is often heralded as the "bible of business strategy" (McNeilly, 2013).

Think about the language we throw around all the time—We're "in the trenches," trying different "tactics" and "guerrilla marketing strategies" to "hit our targets."

"Is that the hill you want to die on?"

"They went into the meeting guns blazing."

"You need to bite the bullet."

The "rules of engagement" for business have been written by men and were inspired by war strategy.

Not only are there echoes of the military in our language, but the military is also at the core of what business is traditionally about:

Beat the competition (i.e., win the war).

Maximize your profits (in war, winners control finite resources and land).

Be tough.

Know your enemy.

Exploit weakness.

7

Frankly, military-inspired business strategy doesn't serve anyone anymore. And it doesn't need to be the foundation on which we grow our businesses.

It's no wonder that fewer than 2% of women in business earn seven figures. We're playing a game we weren't invited to and following a set of rules that were written by white men, who most likely had women at home taking care of the laundry and shopping for groceries.

Let's acknowledge that existing business strategy doesn't serve us and get started creating something new. We can embrace our competitive spirit without needing to crush everyone around us. We can be fiercely ambitious and celebrate other entrepreneurs' success. We can listen to our intuition, while reviewing the hard data.

We don't have to hold ourselves and others to masculine standards that don't serve us. Growing up in a culture where men wrote the rules means that our success is adjudicated by their rules and we judge ourselves (and other women) through their eyes (Beaton, 2021).

The sad thing is that we are so used to being judged through the male lens that we don't even notice.

Interrupting patterns that have been around for millennia doesn't happen overnight. But timing is to opportunity what location is to real estate. And there has never been a better time for women in business. Service-based businesses continue to grow and expand. Technology allows us to work more efficiently and flexibly. The virtual world allows us to expand our potential client base.

We can use the strategies that work for us and dismantle the rest. We can work together. Support each other. Reject the "old boys' club" rules that don't serve us. Grow businesses that feed us (literally and figuratively) *and* become like Madam CJ Walker and use our wealth to influence change.

I want to support all women. To help them uncover their ambition and revel in the freedom entrepreneurship can provide. I love big ideas and innovation. And making plans that result in achieving fantastic goals.

And if we're going to find success in business, we have to take some of the good stuff that men have taught us, trust our instincts, and make our own rules.

Now, who's ready to play?

A SIDE NOTE ABOUT "WOMEN"

When I use the term 'women', I am referring to all people who use that label to describe themselves. While gender non-conforming folks have always been with us, we are in the early days of our collective understanding that gender isn't a binary - male/female, man/woman. That gender is a great big continuum.

At its core, this is a book about women and for women. My hope is that folks who are other genders may also find this guide helpful.

It is also important to note that even if you are a woman, you may not see yourself in all aspects of this book. While gender is a significant factor in our experience, we are multifaceted with a diversity of life experiences, race, religion, ability, education, class, etc that also influence our experiences in the world. Feel free to embrace what resonates with you and reject what doesn't speak to your lived experience!

WELCOME

I see you. You're stumbling out of bed at 4 am after a restless sleep so you can get three hours of work done before you have to make lunches (according to everyone's unique dietary needs) and get the kids out the door. Once they're gone, you throw in a load of laundry, reply to some emails, and pour some lukewarm coffee down your throat. The pressure keeps mounting.

You feel flutters in your chest, and it damn well better be anxiety and not a heart attack because there is no time to see the doctor today.

One of the kids needs something at school, and who do they call? Mom.

The car has to be taken for an oil change, but your partner has a 9–5 job, so it falls on you.

Did anyone remember to call in that prescription? Oh great, out of refills ….

2020 gifted us a global pandemic, the effects of which we're feeling years later, and so those of us who do it all are doing more …

And yet, you're managing to "do it all and more." There's a weird honour to hearing someone say, "I don't know how you do it! You're amazing!" But amazing is not how you feel.

You feel ground down. Flat. Exhausted. With every new request, you feel like you're being pecked to death by chickens.

You're worried about all of the things, at home and at work, but you're pushing through because you refuse to quit. Why? Because you're a leader, the one everyone relies on. In your family, with your circle of friends, and in your business. And because what the hell other choice do you have? You've got bills, mouths to feed, clients to serve. And also, because you want to. You want to grow your business, to serve your clients, to do what you love. You want to create the life you dream about.

Yet, you spend so much time feeling guilty. For the time spent away from your kids. For the time spent working on your business. For the extra unpaid time you put into a client project. For phoning in a client project. So much time in your own head, examining and re-examining your decisions and beating yourself up.

You are the greatest asset in your business. And yet that's not how you treat yourself. (Don't beat yourself up over this, too. Keep reading).

Women are socialized to be caregivers. People pleasers. Selfless mothers.

Nurturing. Kind. Endlessly patient. Accommodating. (Jackson, 2016)

This is what we're taught. From the time we are sorted into pink and blue onesies. These days, much of the gendered messaging is far less overt than it once was, thank goodness. But the messages we learned are deep and ingrained.

In short, we are taught to prioritize everyone else over ourselves.

How do we square this with the fact that, as small business owners, we're the first, and often the greatest, asset we have in our business? Let's look to other sectors where "the person" is the asset.

How about athletes and musicians? A professional athlete knows their career longevity depends on how they care for their bodies. They treat themselves with care, especially if they're not at their best. When they're feeling exhausted or injured, they take appropriate measures. They rest. Without apology.

What do we know about pro athletes? We know that they narrow their focus and really take care of themselves. They exploit their natural talents. They practise to hone their skills. They're getting massages and acupuncture. They're doing ice baths. They're working with physiotherapists. They're doing mindset work. They make it a part of their training to actively take care of themselves because "they" are their career. Pros are their greatest asset.

Athletes also know how to keep going when they're not at peak performance. Playing competitive sports while injured is risky, but people do it anyway. They do it for the Olympic aspirations, for the money, for the love of the game, for personal satisfaction. They do it because their living depends on it.

Professional musicians are the same. Lady Gaga lives with severe chronic pain from fibromyalgia, often experiencing full-body spasms. She has said she doesn't know how other people deal with debilitating illness without the same financial and moral support that she has. But she keeps going.

Just like musicians and elite athletes, the business women I know push through the pain (literal and figurative). We have strong work ethics. We are driven. We have a yearning and a longing for more. We want to be able to perform on our own terms. We're excellent at pushing through because our living depends on it, too. And we love the feeling of winning—of landing a new client, nailing the speaking engagement, or delighting a client.

That's where the similarities end, isn't it? Pro athletes and entertainers are glorified, highly paid, and revered by many. Of course, they should be taking good care of themselves. When they're injured and when they're well.

The world doesn't quite feel the same way about the average woman. And yet, here we are. Less than a hundred years after earning the "right" to be considered people under the law,[1] despite the uneven playing field, women are doing everything men do. We open bank accounts, vote, run empires, lead governments, and change our own tires (if we choose to).

We smash glass ceilings while also raising the floor. We challenge the roles society has written for us and yet, we're still somehow the ones expected to remember that we're out of milk and it's our mother-in-law's birthday.

Why doesn't anyone want our autographs? Why aren't we all millionaires? This is gruelling work. Rewarding? Of course. But it's not a walk in the park. And at the same time, nobody is forcing us to do it. We're doing this because we have a hunger for more.

As ambitious women, if we're going to create our own rules while trying to navigate business in a man's world, we also need a plan to protect ourselves. We have to get clear on the things we need to do to build successful, profitable, sustainable businesses as women. And then? We'll show them what it really means to "run like a girl."

A SIDE NOTE ABOUT AMBITION

If you're reading this wondering, *who is Sara talking to* and asking yourself if you're *wildly ambitious*, take a moment to sit with those thoughts. Does the word "ambition" make you a little uncomfortable? This might be because it can be used as a polite way of judging women for being selfish. Um hum, an excellent example of a characteristic valued in men but not in women. *She Rules* is as much about unlearning the old rules we are taught as it is about embracing new ones.

Ambition is a bold descriptor. So how about this to start? Have you ever been described as a firecracker? Do you have a yearning for more? Are you a go-getter? A self-starter? A doer? Do you have secret desires for success that you haven't told anyone about yet? Yes? You, my friend, are ambitious. So, let's own it. And get on with making it happen.

[1.] The People's Case marks the "historic decision to include women in the legal definition of "persons" was handed down by Canada's highest court of appeal. This gave some women the right to be appointed to the Senate of Canada and paved the way for women's increased participation in public and political life. Though this decision did not include all women, such as Indigenous women and women of Asian heritage and descent, it did mark critical progress in the advancement of gender equality in Canada" (Government of Canada, 2021)

WHY I WROTE SHE RULES

I grew up and married into fishing families. On my dad's side, we are sixteen generations of fishers and trace our fishing roots 400 years back to the Basque region of France. My life has *always* revolved around fishing. About sixteen years ago, large boats from another province started fishing in our region's waters using unsustainable fishing methods. We were worried the herring stocks would collapse like the cod did in the 1990s, which would be terrible for the herring, the ecosystem, and our livelihoods.

It was a big deal—fishers protested with escalating intensity over a three-year period. There were riot police on the wharf, and fishers were arrested. At the beginning of the fourth year of this annual shit show, I formed an organization with three other women called Women for Environmental Sustainability (WES). As an activist group, we had one goal—save the herring stocks—and time was running out.

In the beginning, someone gave me a copy of Saul Alinsky's *Rules for Radicals* (Alinsky, 1971). I loved it and read them over and over figuring out how to apply them. We were relentless. We leveraged political circumstances. We made the government live up to their own rules. We mounted a massive grassroots campaign (before I even knew what that was). And we won.

It took less than six months.

There were many things in our favour, but it was Saul's Rules—our strategy—that laid the foundation on which we built the plan to win.

And, so, when I started in business, I naturally went looking for strategies and advice to help me understand how to succeed in this new world. Sales were not part of my "not-for-profit" job, and I was scared of selling. I could write a proposal for $300,000, but I couldn't ask you for $20 for my kid's raffle tickets.

As a result, one of the first books I read was called *Pitch Anything: An Innovative Method for Presenting, Persuading and Winning the Deal* by Oren Klaff (Klaff, 2011). I've long forgotten the details, but it was full of advice on how to be the alpha at the negotiating table. How to crush the competition. How to appeal to their lizard brain and manipulate situations to win at all costs. It was . . . interesting, but more in a sociological study, "I can't believe people act like this" kind of way. I was horrified by the hierarchical, caveman, chest-beating, militaristic rhetoric.

I wanted to be a high performer, so I binged Tim Ferris podcasts as I walked the beach. I wanted to have big growth, so I read the *10X Rule* by Grant Cardone. And I wanted to figure out how to be a better marketer, so I listened to books and podcasts by Gary Vaynerchuk.

The advice was so full of privilege and devoid of the practical realities of my life—summer childcare to arrange, aging parents to support, back-to-school shopping to be done …

Don't get me wrong, the men have great nuggets of wisdom and strategy we can use, but it wasn't the strategy I needed to deal with the shit that was in front of me each day.

Luckily, I discovered women leaders like Eleanor Beaton. I got business advice that resonated and permission to not make cupcakes for the kids' classes. I learned so much from her podcast that I went on to enroll in two of her programs. The first on podcasting was invaluable as I launched my radio show. And her fantastic program, *Power, Presence, Position* helped me refine my business vision and messaging.

I found Annie Duke's book, *Thinking in Bets: Making Smarter Decisions When You Don't Have All the Facts.* And revisited Laura Vanderkam's body of work, which better speaks to the whole of women's experience. I shouted from the rooftops when I read *Fair Play* by Eve Rodsky, a book that offers practical solutions for the unequal distribution of household labour.

But I couldn't stop thinking about the stats for women in business.

Every business starts at zero, but why do 86% of women-owned businesses get stuck at the hardest stage—making less than $100,000/year? Why are most women grinding it out with none of the freedom or flexibility they dreamed about when they started their business?

How do we move the needle so that more than 12% of us are making $101,000–$999,000/year?

And how do we expand the 2% club—the ones making more than a million dollars a year in annual revenue? It is still groundbreaking for women to achieve significant success in business. How do we turn that path these trailblazers have created into a superhighway, where there are loads of entry points for everyone? And how do we make sure that those who are succeeding are not just middle-class, white women?

Luckily, I didn't have to go far when I started looking for really successful women in business because I've had a front seat view of my dear friend Susan's thirty-year business career.

After decades working as a CFO (Chief Financial Officer) at a number of tech companies, Susan founded her first business in 2012 and sold it in 2018. She sold because she had cofounded another company that needed all of her attention. Numbercrunch provides full-service, outsourced financial solutions. Which, by the way, is an entirely new class of service in the financial space. That she created. So innovative and brilliant.

Her success is not without a multitude of challenges, but I've also observed her uncover her ambition and blaze her own trail—embracing the rules of business that work for her and ignoring the ones that don't. As a result, she's created a company with a diverse workforce that employs more than two dozen people and supports hundreds of small business owners. And she volunteers tirelessly in her business community to support and champion diversity, inclusion, and belonging for entrepreneurs.

Being on Susan's journey with her helped me understand that successful business women are extraordinary . . . and normal people at the same time.

So, when an internet radio station reached out in the summer of 2019, I jumped at the chance to create a radio show/podcast called "Breakthrough." Before the pandemic hit and I had to shift focus, I interviewed two dozen women from all walks of life who hit seven figures and beyond. We had amazing conversations about their businesses, their lives, the obstacles they faced, and the opportunities they identified.

I wanted to know about them. To see if I could see the common themes that revealed a pathway and an action plan so I could replicate their success with my clients . . . and in my own business. How lucky was I to have twenty-four conversations with modern-day trailblazers?

She Rules is a combination and a culmination of those conversations, my deep understanding of women's experiences, and external factors that are always at play. It combines my love of strategy, planning, and business with my practise of changing systems from the inside.

She Rules is a book about business strategy. But more than that, I've created a feminist business strategy. It is leading-edge, fresh, and is designed to help you achieve the business success you dream about, without losing yourself.

Ready to keep going?

— FEMINIST BUSINESS STRATEGY: A PRIMER —

This is a book about feminist business strategy, so let's take a look at what that actually means. I find we often throw around words without having a shared understanding of what they mean. So, I'm going to start by unpacking what I mean by "feminism," "business," and "strategy." Then, I'll pull them together to explain what I mean by a "feminist business strategy." Let's dig in.

FEMINISM: THE SHE RULES DEFINITION

There isn't one area of life that doesn't have a gender lens to it. It touches everything, from our experiences in our families and our social lives to our educational and employment opportunities.

While there are many, many definitions of feminism, mine is this:

Feminism is a belief and a movement that actively works to ensure equal rights and opportunities for women in all areas, at all levels.

I worked for a feminist organization whose mandate was to "increase the status of women on Prince Edward Island," regardless of race, religion, or socio-economic status. Regardless of whether they knew who we were or shared our politics. As a result, I've always taken a "feminism is a big tent" approach. If you see yourself in the movement, then come on in, and get ready to learn (and unlearn).[2]

My feminism is ever-evolving. As the daughter of a second-wave feminist, I grew up in the women's liberation movement, a largely white middle-class women's movement that excluded the voices and experiences of racialized women and 2SLGBTQ+ people. I didn't know at the time that the movement I saw myself and my mother reflected in excluded so many other voices (hello, white privilege). It was uncomfortable to realize this, and I'm thankful for the evolution of this movement and my understanding.

I'm grateful for the third and fourth waves of feminism that pushed me to engage more deeply and critically with the feminist movement and my place in it. Along the way, I've been inspired by Black scholars like Kimberlé Crenshaw, who introduced the concept of intersectionality—how certain aspects of who you are will increase your access to the good things or your exposure to the bad things in life (Steinmetz, 2020).

[2] Over time, I did create a caveat to my "big tent" philosophy: you need to believe that women have the right to have autonomy over their body.

16

It makes so much sense—of course, women's experiences are not the same! Your race, class, socio-economic status, religion, and gender are but some of the overlapping and interdependent systems of discrimination or disadvantage, privilege or advantage you experience.

An intersectional feminist lens is one of ongoing change, growth, discomfort, and transformation. A commitment to actively learning and unlearning and then choosing your path to doing better. It is about being thoughtful and remembering that not everyone has had the same experience as you.

I come from a working-class family in a small rural community. I live with a disability. I'm white, straight, and middle-class (now). These aspects of my experience indicate places where I am more or less advantaged. We likely share similarities and differences in our experience.

FEMINISM AND THE PATRIARCHY

So, what is the patriarchy anyway? It's a complex system of gender politics that enforces strict and outdated norms and rules on our behaviour and the way we interact with one another based on our gender.

Men tend to benefit from patriarchal systems, but they are also held to unreasonable standards. Traditionally the "man box" has been pretty small—they must be strong, unemotional, aggressive, and hyper-heterosexual.

Women are characterized as emotional, maternal, and dependent. Any deviation from these norms can result in judgement, both internal and external. From the perspective of a patriarchal structure, the boxes in which men and women should live are different and tiny.

"Smashing the patriarchy" means observing these societal expectations and working to change them to create a better world for everyone, regardless of your gender, race, religion, ability, or socio-economic status.

BUSINESS: THE SHE RULES DEFINITION

Now that we have a working definition of feminism, let's look at business. Business in its most basic form is the trade and the purchase and sale of products or services to make a profit. Business is fun. It provides an opportunity to stretch and grow. To have flexibility and freedom. To solve problems and create something new.

Business is nested in a capitalist structure. Capitalism is often thought of as an economic system in which individual people or corporations own and control property in accord with their interests. The essential feature of capitalism is the motive to make a profit.

Capitalism creates inequality—we've seen the erosion of the middle class and a greater divide between rich and poor over the past fifty years. It creates billionaires whose wealth is built on the backs of poorly paid workers. Even though we know capitalism creates inequality, it's what we, as a society, have right now.

While there are big players like Amazon and Walmart, the backbone of our economy is small business. Systems are made up of people, including millions of business owners, who can choose to make decisions that are both profitable and work to make the world a better place.

In 2020, during Black Lives Matter, I saw a lot of business owners actively seeking out Black-owned businesses to support and work with. For example, an online group I'm in created a directory of Black-owned marketing businesses—copywriters, web developers, agencies, graphic designers, etc.—that group members could hire for various marketing contracts.

The more we understand our privileges and the inequality in the world and can see ourselves in the change, the more we will use entrepreneurship to work toward that change.

STRATEGY: THE SHE RULES DEFINITION

And, finally, strategy is your cheat sheet. A way to cut through the noise and stay focused and clear on your path forward to accomplish the goals you want for your business and life. It's a combination of the big picture and the details that are going to guide you to where you want to go.

A plan to get you from where you are to a target you want to hit. It keeps you on track, working smart, and with purpose.

For example, you may choose to have a cost strategy, a differentiated product or service strategy, or a focus on a niche strategy. Using a brand most people know, Walmart has built its business by beating the competition based on price. Having the best prices helps them make all their decisions, whether it is where they source their products, how they set up their store, or what brands they carry.

A company like Knix is focused not on price but on creating an innovative solution to an age-old problem. As a business that sells period underwear to women who need them, they are competing directly with well-known sanitary napkin companies but with a significantly different product. Their strategy was to solve the same problem as their competition, but in a very different way.

Business strategy can feel big and dramatic, but it should be simple and expand as your business does. For example, solopreneurs can easily identify their strategy and create a plan in 90 minutes once every 90 days. For example, you can check out my 90 for 90 program at https://sherules.biz.

Strategy can also be reflective of your industry or sector. For example, service-based businesses often bootstrap their growth, which means they self-fund, because the cost to get started is quite low. This means you begin focusing on selling your services to clients pretty quickly because you need the money to fund your business (and lots of other reasons too).

Contrast this to a SaaS business (Software as a Service), where the founder needs to create the software before it can be sold. Let's use Canva as an example. Before the founder of Canva could sell anything, they had to develop the software, test it, refine it, etc., which all costs money. This means that a SaaS business will likely want to focus on product development and finding investors, since they are unlikely to be able to bootstrap the business. In other words, your area of focus and plan of action is different based on your industry or sector.

Other strategies are more universal. When focused on growing a business, others (mostly men) understand they must surround themselves with a strong support team. A partner who stays at home, dry cleaning, laundry service, meal services, housekeepers, fully-serviced apartments or houses, a personal assistant, a manager for their personal stuff.

And they do so unapologetically. Their strategy is to pick a lane, put the blinders on and go for it. Behind every great man . . . and all that. And they don't have it wrong! It is a strategy that works, and it's been working for them for a long time.

The rub is, women don't and can't stick to one lane. We are knocking ourselves out trying to have success while being the player and the support team. We can't win playing by the old rules because they don't apply to us. That's why we need a different strategy.

FEMINIST BUSINESS STRATEGY

The systems we want to change are made up of people, so feminist business strategy focuses on the personal and the world around us—your community, however you choose to define it.

Feminist business strategy is about abundance and freedom. In other words, we want to make money, and we want to do it on our own terms.

Being a woman impacts your experience, and feminist business strategy accounts for the complexity of women's lives. It recognizes and celebrates that our experience in the world is different from men. It honours the whole of you and amplifies your voice. It reminds us that we are working for a better world for all. And that includes doing your part to create the many entry points on the superhighway to seven figures.

Feminist business strategy is about learning and unlearning—the toxic messages that keep us in tiny boxes are everywhere. The more you know, the more you'll see the oppression you've been living with, both external and internal. And the easier it will become to sidestep society's expectations (and your internalized version of them).

And feminist business strategy includes fun. Despite the "angry feminist" stereotype, feminist business strategy is enjoyable, exhilarating, and amazing. As business owners, we're creating the life we want, after all.

And, finally, feminist business strategy is about you. It's about building your confidence, uncovering your unique skills, and fuelling your ambition.

I'm pretty pumped you're on this journey. We're going to dig into the rules now, and I can't wait to see how you apply them.

A NOTE ABOUT MEN

I have a button from my 20s that emerges from time to time that says, "*Men of quality are not threatened by women seeking equality.*"

It is easy to focus on the men who are *not* quality. And for a lot of my career, I did. I raged against the "mediocre white man" who had all the confidence, yet few of the skills of the women who reported to him. The men who are violent. Who harass. Who mansplain. Who pay unequal wages. Who hang out at the old boys' club, making deals that benefit each other. Who attribute their success to hard work with no idea how much privilege they enjoy.

But here's the thing: I am far more hopeful about men these days. While I mostly work with women, the men I know in my business world are all wonderful humans. They are collaborative, thoughtful, and respectful.

Please surround yourself with men of quality. And remember that they grew up in the same patriarchy soup as you—they contend with toxic masculinity, strict boundaries on what is acceptable behaviour, and a general lack of understanding of how much the world caters to their every whim (I'm talking specifically about white men here).

But they want to live in a more equitable world as well. They have learning and unlearning to do. As business owners, they can benefit from employing a feminist business strategy and many of the rules, strategies, and tactics I outline here.

While it's not our job to educate men on how to do better, given the enduring unequal distribution of household labour, everyone should read *Fair Play* by Eve Rodsky. Yep, support women in business by teaching men how to be better partners and fathers.

HOW TO USE THIS GUIDE

This book is designed for you, the one with the stack of unread business and self-help books on your shelf. I encourage you to read the six **She Rules** and, beyond that, flip through the rest of the book. Find the affirmations, applications, tactics, and strategies that speak to you in the moment.

One important note to keep in mind: Many of the exercises and activities in this book are intended for people at different stages of business growth (more about that later in the Make a Plan According to Your Stage of Business section). Some are intended for the early days, while others are better suited for women who have been in business for years. Take what you can from those that apply to you but do read the others to remind and/or inspire you of where you've been and where you're going. I hope you'll come back to this book throughout your business journey, both in good times and in challenging ones.

As a special bonus for buying this book, you can download the accompanying *She Rules Workbook* at https://sherules.biz/workbook

I also hope you'll join the She Rules Facebook Group. I would be delighted to hear from you—how you're using the rules, your wins, and the challenges you're facing as you apply these new rules of business to your world. We will deepen the conversations as we co-create the success the She Rules will bring to all of us.

Finally, there's a section at the back of the book where I list the resources I talk about throughout the book.

Let this be your guide to doing business as an ambitious woman in a man's world. May it inspire and energize you as you build momentum and be your soft place to land on your hard days.

EXPLAINING THE RULES...

SHE RULE ONE: ALIGN WITH YOUR VALUES AND YOUR VISION

I spent eight years working in my dream job—getting paid to be a feminist within an organization that exists solely to improve the status of women in Prince Edward Island (PEI). I mean, it couldn't have been more perfect for me. I was researching, advocating, and making a difference in women's lives. I loved it. We were a small but ambitious team (a common theme in my life), working on a multitude of issues affecting women—domestic violence, creating a community response to poverty, women's leadership, reproductive rights, empowerment, etc.

In 2009, I got to lead the development of Trade HERizons, a program designed to increase the number of women in skilled trades on PEI. I led a team that collaborated with our community, government, private sector, educational institutions, and tradeswomen to address barriers women face in all aspects of the trades sector.

It was amazing work. I got to do all the things I love—use research and evidence (ask me about my favourite research studies) to create a model for improving gender equity in the trades. I got to work with folks who had different opinions and experiences than me to address big and little problems. I got to promote this program, attend conferences, problem solve, walk the shop floors, and help the tradeswomen find their own path to navigating the very fine lines in their world. I got to learn so much!

We were addressing the supply—we created our own career exploration and college prep training programs for women interested in trades. We created posters to hang in high schools, showcasing badass tradeswomen in our community. We encouraged educators at all levels to create more welcoming spaces for women.

We listened to the instructors' worries about how to work with women in ways that were respectful and how to deal with the complexities of women's lives— their male students generally didn't talk about the challenges of securing child-care, needing time off to take their mother to a doctor's appointment, or being sexually harassed at the job placement.

And we were trying to create demand, working with employers and the sector to let them know there was a solution to their ever-growing labour shortage. Less than 5% of tradespeople are women, yet women have great fine motor skills, above-average attention to detail, and they take better care of equipment. And if the employer is good, they stick around.

Sexism, lack of bathroom access, lack of proper fitting PPE, the old boys' net-works, sexual harassment, and the assumptions and realities of the physicality of the trades were a few of the issues we tackled.

It was super hard work but also fun and rewarding. About five years after we started Trade HERizons, a woman from the first group came to my office to show me her last pay stub of the year. She had more taken off in payroll deductions that year than she made on Social Assistance before she started Trade HERizons. Amazing!

The program was supporting women in changing their lives, like that woman who raised herself and her children out of poverty, while working to change the systems to better work for tradeswomen.

When we started Trade HERizons in 2009, the province was on track to see an equal number of men and women in the trades in 276 years. By 2017, through so much combined effort, our researcher was able to estimate that we're now on track to see that number in 45 years. That's going from eleven generations down to one and a half.

In less than ten years, we cut 231 years off the march to gender equality in the trades sector on PEI. How does that *not* get your juices flowing!?

And yet, as exciting as this is, there is still so much work to be done. Retention in the trades sector is dismal because of harassment, sexism, wage inequality, and the lack of job opportunities (despite a shortage of skilled labour). The trades sector being a welcome space for women is still a long way off.

But by 2015, I was feeling burnt out. We completed a big project in 2014 (which I'll talk about later), and the fall of that year brought the beginning of the #MeToo and #TimesUp movements in Canada. The Jian Ghomeshi scandal broke, the Bill Cosby allegations ramped up in intensity, and in Atlantic Canada, we had the Dalhousie University Dentistry scandal (male students were posting misogynistic comments online about women classmates).

While past experience had led me to assume the women I worked with all experienced sexual violence and trauma, there was a particular intensity about that fall. I was experiencing vicarious trauma at a magnitude that was more than I could handle. (Vicarious trauma can result from being repeatedly exposed to other people's trauma and their stories of traumatic events.) My mental health was in jeopardy, and I knew I needed a change.

It was an honour to be part of the patchwork quilt of this beautiful organization that gave me so much as a kid and as a grown up. And it was time for other folks to take the work to the next level, which they've done. As a feminist organization should, Women's Network employs passionate and committed folks who continue to evolve and respond to the changing needs of its community.

Through the leaving process, I realized that the core tenet to my life's work is that I believe gender equality can solve **all** of the world's problems. That's it.

There's still A LOT of work to do. Which means there are a million entry points towards reaching gender equality. I could choose a different one if I wanted to.

For me to be a happy human, I have to do ambitious work that moves the needle closer to gender equality. To ensure that women's voices are heard and respected. That's what alignment looks like for me. And to build a business that works for your life, you must make it a rule to be in alignment.

To understand alignment, we look first at your core values which are principles that you find desirable, important, or even essential. An alignment between your work and your core values produces satisfaction, a sense of happiness and fulfillment. A misalignment can cause everything from minor problems to major disruptions.

What are your core values? What's your vision for the future? What are you working for?

I certainly didn't know my business vision when I started, but it is to earn

27

7 figures a year by helping other women hit their business goals while working no more than thirty hours a week. My desire to help more women hit 7 figures in their business aligns with my core values around gender equality.

That's my vision. That's what I am moving toward. And as opportunities come my way, and as I create my own, that's what I circle back to. *Sara, is this plan/ idea/opportunity in alignment with your values and your vision?*

Alignment allows us to simplify and to keep the important things front and centre so that making decisions is easy. It ensures the work is fun and rewarding because working toward our values and vision is pretty amazing.

You will drift out of alignment, but when you have a guiding north star, you will find your way back more easily.

Sounds great, but how do I know if I'm in alignment? What if I'm out of alignment?

I'm glad you asked! Keep reading for suggestions, exercises, and musings that will help.

Remember you can download the bonus She Rules Workbook at https://sherules.biz/workbook

——————— HOW TO FIND ALIGNMENT ———————

THE TOLERANCE EXERCISE

Grab a piece of paper and a pen, have a big old think, and then write down all the things you're currently tolerating in your business. Don't hold back! Write them all down. . . the big ones and the nit-picky annoying ones. Ask yourself: What am I tolerating? Who am I tolerating? And why am I doing that? What am I doing/not doing as a result?

Consider as well whether you need to reframe. Are there people, circumstances, or situations that need a little more patience and nurturing, rather than teeth-gritted tolerance?

This will quickly help you identify where you need to focus. You'll likely see things that are causing you to drift away from your vision. Catching them quickly allows you to realign with greater ease. And you'll feel better. Who wants to have that fingernails on the chalkboard feeling in business? (I've so dated myself with this reference!) I suggest you add the Tolerance Exercise to your quarterly business review. Things have a habit of sneaking up on you when you least expect it! And as your business grows and changes, you'll find new and exciting things that annoy you.

KNOW WHEN YOUR BUSINESS NEEDS AN EDIT

If the Tolerance Exercise revealed a long list of items, it means that you have some edits to make. There's lots of room for experimentation in the early days when you're keen to make money and pay the bills while learning and refining what you're good at, who you want to serve, and what you like doing.

There will come a time that you'll want to move past your experimental phase. You'll have more answers. The key to sustainable growth is to know when the experimental phase is over and it's time to narrow your focus—you may decide to niche your target audience, your services, or your products, etc. As we grow, it's less about adding and more about making the proper edits—the pruning of the business. I want you to think for a minute: What edits does your business need right now so that you're in alignment?

ADOPT THE FIVE-STAR CLIENT EXPERIENCE

If the Tolerance Exercise or your business edit reveals anything to do with clients, here's a great follow-up for you. Are you tolerating "bad boyfriend" clients? I've borrowed that great expression from my dear friend and fellow entrepreneur, Maureen Hanely. Whether you're straight or not, you know what she means, right? The problem client. The one that drains your energy, sucks up your time, and even steals your enthusiasm for running your business.

A practical strategy for staying in alignment with your vision and your values is to have a five-star client vetting process. This allows you to get really clear on the key things you want to see in the people you work with. In my coaching practice, my five-star client is a woman who is:

★ A service-based business owner

★ Coachable and willing to invest in herself

★ Keen to take action

★ Ambitious with a desire to grow

★ Believes in the power of women supporting women

I know if a potential client ticks these boxes, then we have a great foundation for our work together and that I'm staying true to my business vision. You may choose to work with only 4- or 5-star clients or decide that, as long as a potential customer ticks three boxes, you're happy to proceed.

Much of this depends on your stage of business. If you're early in business, you're still figuring out who you really want to work with, so you're likely to be more flexible. Beware: This level of flexibility can result in "bad boyfriend clients," but that's an important part of the journey ... sifting and sorting to see what you want and what you don't.

I talk to women all the time who can give me a list of what they don't want in a client, which is important, but don't stop there.

When you know what you want:

● The Universe will help out and send clients your way.

● You can speak directly to them through your sales copy, email newsletters, blogs, and social media updates. Marketing is way easier when you know who your five-star client is.

● You'll receive more referrals when your network knows who you work with.

● You'll delight your five-star clients with your onboarding and delivery.

● Your work will be more enjoyable, and you'll make more money.

Final fringe benefit: You'll reduce decision fatigue because you can refer to your list when you're vetting a new prospect and not make decisions from scratch each time.

MOVE THROUGH RESISTANCE

Are some of your business edits feeling harder than others? Do some give you more tension in your shoulders than others?

I recently taught a workshop where one of the women was procrastinating on a simple call to the bank to set up new bank accounts.

Upon reflection, she realized it was because she wanted to use the *Profit-First* model, and she thought the bank would push back on her plan (it requires multiple bank accounts). Once she saw where the resistance was coming from, she was able to quickly take action.

Here's a simple exercise if you're feeling stuck. Ask yourself:

- What am I procrastinating?
- How important is it?
- Where is the resistance coming from?
- Where am I out of alignment?
- What's the one thing I can do right now to move through this?

The more we sit with our resistance, the longer it takes for us to see the growth we want in our life and in our business.

BE LASER-FOCUSED

Remember the herring crisis from the **Why I Wrote She Rules** section: we were successful in our efforts, in part due to our laser focus. There were (and are) a multitude of environmental crises we could have decided to address, but we were all herring, all the time. (That sounds like a Rose Nylund/Golden Girls story from "back in St. Olaf." Another reference to age me if you're playing along).

In the last quarter of 2020, I took a course called "Create Your Online Course in 30 Days Flat" from my entrepreneur friend, Heather Deveaux.

I knew it was my most important business-building activity for the quarter, and I really loved the idea of having a course built and ready in 30 days. When I started, I didn't believe that I could actually do such a thing in a month, but I did. Because I adopted and employed a laser focus. For the month of

November, I did client work and built out my course. Laser focus means being explicit about what you are focusing on, as well as what you are intentionally pausing (bookkeeping, onboarding process development, etc.). It helped that there were accountability calls and support from Heather for the moments when I was certain the timelines were impossible.

Stop and think about one thing that would make the biggest difference in your business right now and focus on that one thing until it's done. Then move on to the next. If you make a point of spending 80% of your focus on those activities for the next 90 days, you'll see the change that you want. Shameless plug time: My coaching program, "7-Figure Confidence" helps you do just this. You can learn more at SheRules.biz.

FOLLOW THE 80-20 RULE

A companion to being laser-focused in your business is applying the 80–20 rule. The 80–20 rule means that 80% of your outcome is derived from 20% of your effort. For example, in general, 20% of your customers represent 80% of your sales. And 20% of your time produces 80% of your results. And so on.

The Pareto Principle, or "80/20 Rule" as it is frequently called today, is a great tool for growing your business. For instance, if you can understand which 20% of your time produces 80% of your business' results, you can spend more time on those activities and less time on others. Likewise, by identifying the characteristics of the top 20% of your customers (who represent 80% of your sales), you can find more customers like them and dramatically grow your sales and profits.

Don't believe this can possibly be accurate? You can look at your own business to see which customers, services, or products are producing the bulk of your revenues. For example, a copyeditor reviews her financial reports and discovers that 80% of her revenues are coming from her editing services for memoirs, which is one of five services she provides. While representing 20% of the services she offers, editing for memoirs equals 80% of the money coming in.

This exercise gives her important information. She could choose to focus her marketing efforts on building out her other service offers, or she could go all in on memoir editing and focus her efforts there. When you know what your optimal service or products are, this is where you focus. And the rest? That's where you can edit if you want.

Using this principle, you could cut 80% of your activities and still see success. Terrifying? Yes. And true. In one of my Breakthrough Podcast episodes, Kathy Robertson of Robertson Wealth Advisory Group shared her experience of using the 80–20 rule to increase profitability and reduce her workload and expenses. Over 18 months, she trimmed her client roster from 500 to 180. Integral to that process was determining if the top 20% of clients were the folks she wanted to work with.

Another guest, Martha van Inwegen (Founder, President, and Chief Alchemist of Life Elements, Inc.), scaled her business to 7 figures by cutting all but one product from her line of natural beauty products.

Applying the 80–20 rule is relevant if you've been in business for some time and you have the data to explore. If you're still in the early stages, you can relax on this one. But be mindful of it because at some point, it will come into play for you!

KNOW YOUR NON-NEGOTIABLES

One thing that we want to be mindful of, as we grow our businesses from a place of alignment, is knowing what our non-negotiables are. And we usually learn those non-negotiables by doing things that don't feel good.

A clear boundary for me is that I only work with women business owners. Over the years, I've worked with a few men to help them grow their business, but it just wasn't a good fit. I have a deep understanding of women's experiences, allowing me to lean into all of my skills and expertise. This also aligns with my desire to support more women in growing their businesses and personal wealth. I was pretty sure I only wanted to work with women, and by working with men, I was able to confirm it. Can I coach men? Sure. But I shine when I coach women.

What are your non-negotiables? Some people only work certain hours of the day, some are not willing to travel, and others have clear boundaries on the types of employees they hire. It's helpful to think about your own. Do you have any that are aspirational? For me, I aspire to continue to build my morning routine to include a consistent meditation practice that I can't live without.

Take a few minutes to imagine your non-negotiables and write them down.

FIND YOUR ZONE OF GENIUS AND THEN FIERCELY PROTECT IT

In his groundbreaking book, *The Big Leap*, Gay Hendricks teaches us to think about the things we do in our lives and categorize them in four ways. He shows how we spend our lives going among different zones—incompetence, competence, excellence, and genius.

Finding your zone of genius . . . and then fiercely protecting it is an iterative and ongoing process. And it is absolutely critical if you want to grow your business. But, first, let's understand each zone that Hendricks developed.

- The zone of incompetence: In this zone, you engage in something you inherently do not understand or are not skilled at.

  In a business context, as early-stage entrepreneurs, we often work in our zone of incompetence. This is when you spend three hours trying to upload your blog because you can't afford to hire someone to do it for you (or you believe that you can't afford it).

  Knowing your zone of incompetence helps you understand what you need to outsource first . . . or what you need to learn to become competent or even excellent.

- The zone of competence: In this zone, you do what you are efficient at, but you recognize that many people are likewise efficient at it, and so your capabilities do not stand out in any significant way.

  These are the tasks in your business that are important but don't have to be done by you. Anyone can pick up printer ink, reconcile your books, or even manage aspects of your onboarding process.

  With this zone, it is still relatively easy to see the tasks that don't make sense for you to do. For example, I *can* send my own newsletter, but it makes more sense for me to create the content and hand the proofreading, design, and delivery off to my team.

- The zone of excellence: In this zone, you do something you are tremendously skilled at. Often, the zone of excellence is cultivated, practiced, and established over time. Those skills that were in your zone of incompetence can become your zone of excellence over time. This is the trickiest area. As we grow and build our business, we become better and better at lots of things and then fall into the trap of imagining we are the only ones who can manage our team or sell our products or do our financial analysis or [fill in the blank here]. But just because you are very good at logistics doesn't mean you can't hire a project manager or empower your team to create their own project plans. You don't have to do all of the things.

In my Breakthrough interview with Trivinia Barber, CEO of Priority VA, she shared her struggle getting out of her zone of excellence. As a former virtual assistant, she was brilliant at finding cheap airline flights, but as CEO, this was not where her time was best spent. Even if it was fun. She was good at it. And she enjoyed doing it. Spending time in her zone of excellence pinched off opportunities to uncover and relax into her zone of genius.

- The zone of genius: In this zone, you capitalize on your natural abilities, which are innate, rather than learned. This is the state in which you get into "flow," find boundless inspiration, and produce work that is unique and beyond what anyone else is doing. AKA, you're in alignment.

Your success and happiness hinges on how much time you spend in your zone of genius, even though you're going to flow through these zones in your business regularly. And the amount of time you spend in your zone of genius can depend on where you are in your business.

For example:

My client Kerry Anne owns a 7-figure marketing agency with her business partner. She focuses solely on the creative and brand aspects, which is her zone of genius. She meets with clients and helps the creative team develop brand briefs and high-level concepts. She continues to weave through the zones Hendricks describes, but the bulk of her day is spent in her zone of genius.

Sounds dreamy right? It really is—and she's able to do that because she has a team to support her. Back when her business was a quarter of the size, she was in her zone of genius less because she also had to write web copy, make social media posts, and pick up the mail. Your genius work helps you grow, and you grow because you get help so that you can do more zone of your genius work.

In other words, you need to hit the $75K revenue target to hit the $250K mark to get to 7 figures and beyond. Along that journey, you'll weave through those zones. Your business path, full of peaks and valleys, helps you understand what makes you magical and uniquely you. It takes courage to confidently embrace your talents, and vulnerability to ask for help and admit you're not brilliant at all things.

Finding and fiercely protecting your zone of genius is how you build a business that is in alignment. So, if you are stuck, it's probably because you need to carve out more time for your genius work—your area of expertise. For example, if editing reports bogs you down, hire an editor to review the work before it lands on your desk. You'll cut down the time it takes for you to edit reports, and you'll also carve out just a little more space for the work that only you can do.

KNOW IF YOU'RE GRINDING OR GROWING

Less than 2% of women-owned businesses have more than a million dollars in revenues each year, and 86% of all women-owned businesses make less than $100,000/year. I'm repeating this because it needs attention. Approximately 86% of you are still in start-up mode, which is the hardest stage of business.

When you start a business, regardless of your expertise, you've got a lot to figure out—what kind of marketing you need to do, length of your sales process, client delivery, onboarding, offboarding, invoicing, cash flow . . . the list goes on and on. Which means lots of hard work, long days, late nights, and weekend work.

We tend to think of the start-up phase as time-bound, but much of the time, if you're making less than $100,000/year, it's likely you're clinging to a world where you're doing it all yourself (cause you think you can't afford not to). Which means you're being torn from (see the **Find your Zone of Genius** section) to do all the other parts of the business. Sure, these tasks need to happen for your business to function, so you tell yourself you need to do them. This is simply not true. You are grinding it out—taking the slow, dull, and laborious path.

It's tricky, though, because many of the women I know love to work. And we associate hard work with success. And we're told to put other people's needs before our own. So how do you know the difference between working hard to grow your business and grinding it out?

You've got a deadline. Something unexpected hits (like, say, a global pandemic), and you have to lay off staff or dive deeper into the operations of your business than you have in years. You've said yes to a lot of work, and now you have to *get it done*. There are times, regardless of your company revenues, that you grind it out.

Most seasoned entrepreneurs wear their ability to get stuff done as a badge of honour. They trade "war stories" and are skeptical of "get rich quick" schemes because they know there's no way to skip the hard work of growing a business. They celebrate the grind when they make decisions based on experience and their instincts. But they sure don't *miss* the grind.

Grinding it out is a normal part of business, *but* a whole lot of us are staying stuck in the start-up/less than $100K/year phase much longer than we need to.

What to do if this feels like you?

Ask yourself what you could do to move more quickly through the "grinding it out" times in your business. One idea: You can hire a slice of an experts' time—bookkeepers, copywriters, virtual assistants, accountants, online business managers. You do not have to do it all, nor should you.

If you don't want to spend money, you can ask for help. My mom typed notes for me when I first started out. She also washed my dishes on occasion and helped with kid sports and music lesson logistics. You can make a trade. I traded business coaching for social media support when I couldn't afford to pay for it, and it wasn't in my zone of genius.

Focus on the revenue-generating work you can produce, not how much it is going to cost to pay someone to enter receipts into your bookkeeping software.

If you're feeling that grind right now, try taking a minute to jot down some thoughts of gratitude to remind you of the good things and what you're working towards.

I get it—there can be a lot to hold us back. And sometimes it's external factors, and sometimes it's you. Growing means letting go of perfection. Of needing to do everything yourself. It means imperfect action. So, as your ambitious friend, I offer gentle encouragement to look carefully and evaluate if you're grinding or growing.

HIRE SMART PEOPLE

Hiring the right team members (contract or staff) is even more important than choosing those five-star clients. My uncle Sandy was an electronics salesman, and, over his 30-year career, he sold ¾ of a billion dollars' worth of electronics in this country. Holy snap, that's a lot! When I started my business, I asked him for advice. He said, "Hire people who are smarter than you, then get out of their way and let them do their job."

I've embraced this advice. Make no mistake: Uncle Sandy was always the smartest person in the room because he was a humble leader who embraced and championed a solid team of subject matter experts. And I added my own twist: Make sure your team members are in alignment with your vision and that their values are in sync with your own.

BE FLEXIBLE, EXCEPT WHEN YOU'RE NOT

When I worked in the not-for-profit sector, I always used to say, "My work is flexible, except when it's not." I loved being able to work from home, to easily be responsive to my kids' needs, and to work early in the morning when my brain is most fresh. I've been lucky to have this life/work harmony for many years.

I also lived in a world where the premier's office would call, inviting us to a press conference with a few hours' notice; where a government official we were lobbying (for one issue or another) offered only one meeting time; and where a funder requested a proposal in 48 hours. In those cases, there was no flexibility. You cleared your schedule because it was part of the territory. Sometimes, you just gotta get shit done. Hence, be flexible, except when you can't.

I've carried this philosophy into business, and it's one of the greatest benefits to being your own boss and building a business that you love! And so those times when you've got a deadline or when things are feeling crunchy, that's okay. It's okay to have things that are flexible except when they're not. Especially if you build in the flexibility you most enjoy. I don't do any meetings before 9:30 these days, but there are absolutely folks I'd take an 8:00 call from!

DON'T SELL YOUR SOUL

Many years ago, when I was making about $40,000 a year, I had a conversation with someone who had just received a six-figure job offer. I had dollar signs in my eyes and was so excited for her! Imagine my surprise when she said, "I'm not going to take the job."

I couldn't quite wrap my head around that. On the surface, it was a slam dunk, simple decision. But for her, the job offer was from a company that makes military supplies, which was something she didn't align with her values. She didn't take the job.

She was firm enough on her beliefs to make that decision with ease. Clarity is freedom.

As your business grows, you'll have a lot more people reaching out and asking for your time. And the reality is you also still have to run your business and grow. Know your values and your vision so that you can stay focused on that end goal.

The truth is, when you're a woman in business, particularly as you hit the rare air of $500,000K+, you're going to end up saying no to far more opportunities than you say yes to. It will get easier with practise to see the natural alignments and the easy nos.

SHE RULE TWO: PLAY HURT LIKE A PRO

In August 2017, I was transitioning to full-time entrepreneurship. I wasn't in great health, not sleeping well, and fairly stressed (in hindsight). As I was driving home from work one day, I had a terrible dizzy spell and ended up in the ditch. I didn't hurt myself and I didn't hurt the car, but sometimes the Universe whispers and sometimes it roars. This minor accident on a country road was the roar that changed my life and led me to write this book.

You see, I live with chronic illness and wild ambition. I have Meniere's Disease, which is an imbalance of the fluid in the inner ear. It causes dizzy spells, ringing in the ear, hearing loss and super-sensitive hearing at the same time (strange but true), and deep, deep exhaustion when it's episodic. It's been an unwelcome recurring character in my life for almost 35 years (save for a blissful ten-year period of dormancy when my kids were little).

For a long time, I tried to hide and deny my illness, but after that accident, I decided to surrender to both my illness and my ambition. I've focused on creating a life that I want. In that time, I've doubled my revenues each year, hired a team to help on my sick days and with the things I don't do well, created boundaries, learned how to look after myself, and lost 80 pounds along the way.

I've done this by living what I teach my clients: You create a profitable, sustainable, successful business by focusing on treating you (the business owner) with care. You are a great asset to your business and should be treated as such. Couple that with a solid plan, and you can hit those big goals you have for yourself and your business.

When the world shut down in March 2020, my friend Susan and I made a pact to double down on our self-care. As I mentioned, Susan has a big team and even more clients, who all needed a lot of extra support during COVID.

Like many, we knew COVID was going to be a tough hill to climb and that we needed to be at our best. Little did we know then that COVID would be followed with massive social unrest, a recession disproportionately impacting women, and an uneasiness in re-entering the world again.

By September 2020, so many clients, friends, colleagues, and mentors were reporting feeling exhausted, depressed, anxious, and generally overwhelmed by everything, and yet feeling like they needed to keep pressing forward. Did any business owner actually take a vacation in 2020?

The curious thing was, I was doing okay. Don't get me wrong—there were lots of hard times—but in general, I was doing all right. And, so, with every important life event since we were four, Susan and I talked it through and realized that our self-care practices didn't prevent the hard days but helped us bounce back more quickly.

I love to strategize, support, and advise women on how to grow their business, but I tend to be private about my own struggles with Meniere's Disease. However, I realized that the strategies and practises that I used to manage my illness and grow a business were the very practises that were helping me through the shitshow that was 2020.

So, I started writing these things in my journal that became the basis for this book. I wanted to share my experiences with you because things *are* hard sometimes, and you don't have to go it alone.

I changed my life because the Universe roared at me in my car. In the ditch.

The Universe also:

Whispers

Clears her throat

Speaks sternly

Gives you the side-eye

Pokes you in the back

Raises her voice

Then roars.

You don't have to wait until the roar to make tiny changes that stack up to big wins.

Here are some of my best tips for playing hurt like a pro. And of course, chronic illness or not, we all play hurt at times.

Remember you can download the bonus She Rules Workbook at https://sherules.biz/workbook.

———— HOW TO PLAY HURT LIKE A PRO ————

PRACTICE "FIRST" AID (PUT YOURSELF FIRST)

It's hard to put ourselves first. As women, hurt or not, we are socialized through media messages, school, family expectations, and experiences in the workplace to put the needs of others ahead of our own. Over the past several decades, we are more aware of gender roles, but it doesn't mean we still don't play them out (reminder: Women take on the bulk of household responsibilities, despite working outside the home in similar numbers to men).

Our world is built and operates on the unpaid labour of women. So when you put yourself first, you are seriously pissing off the patriarchy. You are rocking the foundations on which our society was built. It is a radical act to practise "first" aid.

Self-care needs a rebrand. It is seen as self-indulgent and selfish. A hobby of the privileged. And is generally characterized as being about yoga and spa days. While self-care means taking care of yourself so that you can be healthy and happy, needing self-care is seen as weak.

When in fact, it's super badass to dismantle oppressive structures, and that is what you are doing when you choose to put your own needs ahead of others. You are refusing to devalue your time, your skills, and your life … one bubble bath, disc golf round, spa day, long walk, music festival, and guided meditation at a time.

How will you rebrand self-care in your own life?

BE KIND, GENTLE, AND FIRM WITH YOURSELF

A strategy I recommend all the time is to be kind and gentle and firm with yourself. Sometimes we have hard days—clients are unhappy, we're not feeling well, the weight of the world's problems feel especially crushing, and we have PMS. That's a lot, so on those days, we need to be kind and gentle with ourselves.

What does that look like? First, you need to listen to your body. What is it saying? And what does it need? Do you need to pee? Eat some food? Do you need to rest? Go outside? Drink a glass of wine? Call a friend for tea and sympathy? Whatever it is, listen to your body and be gentle with yourself. Kind and gentle is for when just getting through the day is the goal. Firm is for the next day (or week).

I follow James Clear's advice from *Atomic Habits* and have a policy to not skip two days in a row with my good habits. For me, walking outside is important. If I'm really feeling miserable, maybe I won't go for a walk one day, but on the second day, I'm firm with myself and force myself to go outside because I know it will make me feel better in the end. Be kind and gentle and firm. (PS: Sometimes, depending on what's up, you may need long periods of mostly kindness with dashes of firm here and there.)

When it comes to others, of course, we want to treat them with kindness.

(It's not a coincidence that a variation of the "do unto others as you would have them do unto you" rule is found in every religion). Of course, we want to be gentle with people—we have no idea what is happening in other people's lives, but it is safe to assume they are playing hurt in some capacity, at least some of the time, too.

And being firm? Well, this one is tricky because of gender stereotypes.

You are far more likely to be considered a hardass than a man will be. His assertive is your bitchy. So being firm will likely present excellent opportunities to practise this mantra, "what other people think of me is none of my business."

In my experience, despite the risks, people tend to operate better with boundaries and appreciate transparency and accountability. I certainly do.

SET 7-FIGURE BOUNDARIES

Ambitious women have boundaries, even though that also bucks stereotypes. To create boundaries, you have to get comfortable with saying no, which can be really hard! I'm an extrovert, and I love processing out loud. I can get really excited about something in the moment, eagerly say yes, and then upon later reflection, think, ***"Why did I think that was a good idea? Future Sara is going to be so pissed."***

Now when I find myself in that sort of situation, where my inner eager puppy is jumping up and down, my answer is always, ***"Let me think about that, and I'll get back to you."*** It's a great way for me to create a boundary between me and my future self!

If saying no comes easy to you, great! But I had to teach myself not to make decisions about my time in the moment. This allows me to create boundaries with others.

Recently, I had a situation arise where I was tempted to turn my back on the boundary I'd imposed. I'm doing some fun work with a client, helping to develop a 90-day plan to manage what's in front of her right now, while creating a strategy and charting the path she'll follow to achieve her big, bold goals that are three years out. We'd planned a team meeting on a particular date, but I later realized that I offered up a day that I had already booked to spend a rare day off with friends. She decided to go ahead with the team meeting, which made perfect sense.

Three times, I caught myself almost offering to start my friend date later in the day so I could attend the meeting. I had to remind myself over and over that I don't make these kinds of decisions in the moment. In the end, I decided that if the business owner was more than willing to respect my holiday-time boundary, then I should too!

When you're ambitious and playing hurt, boundaries are especially important. We need to focus, and the more successful we become, the more requests we'll get for our time. It's okay to have boundaries, and it's okay to say no.

Although "no" is a complete sentence, it's hard to say on its own, isn't it? We still like to be helpful, so we can offer other solutions. Saying, "I'm not able to present at your workshop; however, this person would do a great job" might feel more comfortable to you than simply saying "No, I'm not available" (even though that second option is a legitimate option).

Creating boundaries gets easier with time, and this is why She Rule One is so important. When you're in alignment and have clarity, this all becomes easier.

GO OUTSIDE

We are an outdoors family. My husband makes his living on the water. He loves to snowmobile and hang out at a cabin in the woods he built with his friends (Yes, they are all in their 40s and 50s … it's both hilarious and sweet). I've always enjoyed summer, but the rest of the seasons? Meh. (I live on the east coast of Canada, which means we get all kinds of weather.) Over the past few years, I've added in nature every day, and my attitude is always better for it. Whether it's a beach walk, snowshoeing, picking chanterelles, or harvesting wild blueberries, I love the outdoors, and it's an integral part of my life. I love it less when it's a blinding blizzard, but with the right gear, it's not that bad.

Try it yourself! I am surrounded by nature, so it is easy for me. It may take a little more effort depending on where you live, but it's worth it. Cities have great parks that you can explore. Create a little bird feeder in your backyard. My friend Fred turned a tiny plot of land outside his London apartment into a garden oasis twenty years ago. He made his own nature in a giant city.

Regardless of what you do, being outside is restorative and usually provides clarity to the problems you face. You can suffer away at your computer for hours, or you can try a walk in a park or around the block. I promise it will be much more fruitful.

ENSURE YOUR GOOD HABITS OUTWEIGH THE BAD

I'm never here to judge anyone's bad habits (we all have them). But here's the deal: In order to grow, you need to nail the basics. Eat well, exercise (particularly outside!), and develop a mindfulness practice. What that looks like will ebb and flow as your needs change. Do you smoke a joint or have a drink and indulge in chocolate? That's entirely up to you. Think about the good habits and the not-so-great habits and keep a consistent measurement to make sure the good habits outweigh the bad.

GET HELP WHEN YOU NEED IT

It's important to seek help. And to push through any baggage you have around getting help, whether that comes from what you put on yourself or from other people. I get a lot of help for managing my Meniere's disease. I don't even think about it anymore, but I see my ear, nose, and throat specialist four times a year. I have a hearing aid. I get massages. I see a Chinese medicine doctor for acupressure. I have done meditation training, hypnosis, and energy work. Some things may work for you for a while, and then you don't need it or want it anymore—that's fine, just move on to something else. (I realize there is a lot of privilege in that sentiment, including being Canadian, where we have access to universal healthcare that pays for some of the treatments I access.)

When you're playing hurt and ambitious, getting help in your business is paramount. I have lots of help now, including an online business manager who keeps me and my business organized, helps me plan, and manages the contractors and staff team.

What's your version of this? If you're feeling ground down by the pandemic (or whatever), there is no shame in seeking help for the mental health challenges that you face. On the business front, I'm a coach, so, of course, I'm going to tell you that you should get help. You can't read the label from inside the bottle, so getting an external perspective on your business is one of the most important things you can do when you are in growth mode.

WE ALL HAVE OUR OWN SHIT
TO DEAL WITH

For me, it's Meniere's Disease. For you maybe it's a physical issue, maybe it's a marital issue, maybe it's a kid issue, maybe it's an ailing parent, maybe it's all of those (and if it is, I'm really sorry!) ... we all have things that make it that much harder to run our business at times.

While we don't want to "borrow trouble," knowing there are strategies you can rely on when things go sideways can be comforting.

If you're playing hurt right now, stay on this section a little longer. Don't worry about the other bits. You may have to focus on survival for a while and that's okay. In order to thrive, you gotta survive first. Narrow your focus. Be ruthless with your time. Take care of you first, no matter how uncomfortable it feels.

CONTINUE...

STORY TIME CONTINUED...

The biggest lesson I've taken from living and growing a business while playing hurt is that you can do more than you think you can. And conversely, that you can tap out more often than you think you can. The delicate balance lies in knowing when to lean in and when to lean out.

Playing hurt also gives other people a chance to help out. I used to hate asking people for help. Now, I just dislike it. But I've learned that team members are often eager for more responsibility, and family, friends, and colleagues are happy to jump in if you need them.

Recently a friend asked if I'd facilitate a session for her because her husband was unexpectedly gravely ill. Not only did I jump at the opportunity to do something tangible to help her during a difficult time, but I would have walked over hot coals to get there. I assure people feel as fiercely about you.

I promise it will get better. All of this gets better. The challenges you face as you play hurt (especially if you have an illness) may still happen. I still get dizzy, but I'm so much better equipped to deal with that was because of my feminist business strategy and the She Rules that ground me.

SHE RULE THREE: BE WILLING TO ADAPT AND CALIBRATE

One thing we rarely learn from business books is how to manage those messy parts of life that women have to figure out when we're running a company and a household. It's frustrating when we're fired up and want more, but life gets in the way. Because no matter how good our intentions or how solid our strategic plan is, sometimes menopause gifts us with insomnia, parents need heart surgery, and teenagers get their hearts broken.

If you also happen to live with a chronic illness, care for an elderly parent, or have a child with special needs, this rule (and all of these rules, truthfully) is going to be particularly critical. To thrive in business, we have to be willing to adapt and calibrate when things aren't working for us, rather than wallow and martyr ourselves.

To borrow an example from my own life, I've come to learn that a slow start to the day is more likely to set me up for success and to not experience dizziness. My children, however, need to be driven to the school bus at 7 am each day.

Historically, that drive to the bus has been shared between me and my partner. In 2020, the pandemic put our kids out of school for six months. While that time with the teenagers at home presented challenges (which would have been much more challenging if they were still babies), I delighted in the slow mornings. Suddenly, there was no more having to race out of the house so early. On the rare times during that period when I had to sprint into action quickly in the mornings, I felt terrible. The pandemic helped me understand I couldn't and wouldn't do it anymore. It gave me clarity that frazzled mornings can trigger a dizzy day.

In preparation for the kids returning to school, I talked to my husband and let him know that I was taking myself out of the early morning drive to school rotation. I have a good partner, and he fully supported the decision, but habits take time to break.

The first two weeks were hard. He would forget and ask, "Are you driving the kids today?"

"No, Scott, remember? I'm not doing that anymore."

I knew my decision was putting some extra strain on him. In the past, I would have shared the load, regardless of the potential impact on me. But this time, I didn't, and, by November, no one even thought of it anymore. It became an established rule that I don't drive the kids to school in the morning.

As women, we're socialized to put others' needs in front of our own—if you have children, they should be first. If you don't, then you should bear more of other family responsibilities. In circumstances like this, our needs are not even part of the equation. We'll whisper a string of curse words under our breath, and out loud we say, "Fine, I'll do it." It doesn't matter if it stacks the odds against me. I need to help out.

This is a shining example of where putting myself first is actually a benefit to my whole family, even when or if it appears selfish. Because I'm making my health a priority, I'm a more enjoyable mother, partner, and housemate.

As I said before, we have to be willing to adapt and calibrate when things aren't working for us. Just like the decision I made to leave a job I loved because it was no longer making me happy.

You, your life, and your business are always changing. A key to successful growth is learning to adjust to changing situations on the fly. And one joy of being a small business owner is our ability to be quick and light as circumstances change.

Remember, even when we know what our North Star is, that doesn't mean we'll always stay on course. Drifting is natural and to be expected (Shiny Object Syndrome is a thing!). But by learning to adapt and calibrate, you can course-correct before you get too far away from your vision or values.

So, what does this look like in practise? It looks like action, reflection, and adaptation.

The willingness to adapt and calibrate allows for experimentation and playfulness. Clarity is a lovely consequence of moving quickly but stopping often to reflect and make changes if necessary. To see what's working and what's not working in your business.

Action with reflection and adaptation builds confidence. You stack wins, you course correct, and you build a business that works for your life. And you don't lose yourself in the process.

You can apply this principle to both the big and little moments of life and business. When you know what your plan is, you measure against it, and make any changes you may need to make to hit your big goals.

Sometimes we need to recalibrate on the fly. It's okay to look at your calendar and decide what can get cancelled or moved, so you can adjust.

The great thing about this She Rule is that the more we use it, the more we build accuracy into our business. The more we focus on our vision and values and create solid plans to measure against, the more likely we are to stay the course.

In the following section, I've included some exercises and ideas to help you drop this She Rule into your own business.

Remember you can download the bonus She Rules Workbook at https:sherules.biz/workbook.

HOW TO ADAPT AND CALIBRATE

MAKE A PLAN ACCORDING TO YOUR STAGE OF BUSINESS GROWTH

There are two key factors to ambitiously growing your business while creating the life you want: Solid self-care and a good plan. An entrepreneurial plan teaches you to adapt and calibrate. It gives you clear direction on what's working and what's not. It helps you quickly identify where you're going off track and gives you the opportunity to find your way back by making small and subtle adjustments. Or blowing the whole thing up, if that's what's called for!

When I talk to groups about planning, some folks will say they find the process restrictive. But I promise you there is nothing more exciting than having a plan that bakes growth and change into the DNA of your business. Being a small business owner gives you the joyous ability to be nimble and to seize opportunities that present themselves. An entrepreneurial plan allows you to do all of that with ease,—not because it constrains you, but because you can make informed decisions about what is working and not in your business. The first step is knowing your Stage of Business Growth.

I always start with understanding my client's stage of business because being clear on your stage of business helps you know exactly what you need to do to move to the next one. One of my favourite models for figuring this out is Todd Herman's Stages of Business Growth (Herman, 2019). At each stage, he breaks down common experiences, poses questions to ask yourself, warns of pitfalls to avoid, and, most importantly, provides growth activities to focus on. You can check out the resources section at the back of this book to learn more about this model.

It is a cheat sheet for avoiding overwhelm, normalizing your experience, and understanding the key activities you need to do to *grow* your business. Re-read that last sentence. You don't have to go through the effort of figuring it all out yourself. As you read *She Rules*, I hope you'll consider the stage of business you're in and take what's applicable to you right now. It will help you get to that next stage with more ease.

IDENTIFY YOUR KNOWN UNKNOWNS

In the world of business planning, we want to account for the things we know could impact us, even when we're unclear to what degree. Part of entrepreneurial planning is understanding the "known unknowns" in your business.

Known unknowns are the risks that an organization is aware of, but is unaware of the size and potential effect of the risk. For instance, the organizers of my favourite music festival (I love you, Stanfest) know there's a risk that rain may affect the event. But the lack of knowledge about how much rain there will be makes it hard to make concrete plans. So, they have a plan and some contingencies.

Meniere's disease is the known unknown in my life. I know it's there. But what's unknown to me is when it's going to flare up and when it's going to leave me alone. I now know the pattern: Between the months of June and October, I'm more likely to feel unwell. So, I tend to plan a little lighter in the summertime. It allows me to both enjoy our beautiful Prince Edward Island summers and to give myself some grace if I'm dizzy. I do this purposefully now, but it took years to truly see the pattern and plan for it.

Thinking about known unknowns as you're doing your planning is important. We tend to have unrealistic expectations for how much we can do in a day, yet underestimate what we can accomplish in a year.

It's good practise to plan for the unexpected and be prepared to recalibrate. What does that look like in practise? As we were developing Trade HERizons at Women's Network, I found Tuckerman's Model of Group Development that explains how healthy teams grow over time. Tuckman's model identifies the five stages through which groups progress: forming, storming, norming, performing, and, hopefully, transforming.

After a few years of running these programs, I knew that the groups would have a conflict (the 'storm" phase) about 3–5 weeks into the programming, so as I was doing my planning, I would make those weeks a little bit lighter. I knew I was likely to have to support staff through some kind of crisis. I didn't know what it would be, but I knew I had to build in time to deal with it.

Stop and have a little think about the known unknowns in your life and business. A good place to start is to identify what you change often and why. Building a management strategy for these unknown risks in your regular planning process is going to help you adapt and calibrate with more ease. And, heck, if the thing doesn't happen, you've got a light week or season—okay!

A LITTLE GARDEN PATH ABOUT UNKNOWN UNKNOWNS

These are the risks that come from situations that are so unexpected that they would not be considered. Small business owners don't have time, energy, or resources for planning for things like COVID-19. It rots when we are blindsided by a global pandemic, but don't beat yourself up for the massive impacts you may have experienced in your business due to something you could have never predicted or planned for.

USE TEMPLATES, MODELS, AND FRAMEWORKS

Regardless of your stage of business growth, templates, models, and frameworks are your friend. Despite the common mythology, business does not have to be hard, and it doesn't have to be complicated. And you don't have to do it all alone.

As women with large lives, we need simple businesses. Templates, models, and frameworks create simplicity. They are generally created by subject-matter experts and are based on their experience, research, and evidence. We don't have time to become experts in all business-building activities, so take the pass every time you can.

While we live in a world of amazing innovation, there is rarely anything all that revolutionary happening. Website sales pages are based on age-old, long-form advertising techniques developed in the early days of advertising. Way back in 2004, a woman by the name of Maria Veloso wrote a book called *Web Copy that Sells,* and the step-by-step formula holds up today.

In big and little ways, you can use models, frameworks, and templates to guide and streamline your business, so make them your friend and put them to work!

LEARN TO AVOID CONTEXT SHIFTING

Have you ever had those moments in your business when you're driving home at the end of the day (or in "work a home" context, you're walking away from your computer) and you think, "I haven't stopped all day and yet, I don't feel like I actually accomplished anything?" Yes? You likely have been the victim of context shifting.

Context shifting is the time lost when you shift your focus between projects. Researchers have found that we lose 20% of our time to shifting between projects. If you've got five projects on the go, you're actually only spending about 5% of your time on each project and 80% of your time shifting between them. Look, app developers spend billions of dollars a year figuring out ways to distract us. Kids, cats, dogs, social media, social unrest, clients … You can easily create a list of what distracts you.

When you're still looking to hit big goals, you need to limit those distractions. In your day-to-day, turn off your notifications, close your office door, and turn off your phone when you're doing deep work.

In the bigger picture, only work on one or two projects per quarter to drive business growth because the more projects we have, the less time and attention we have to focus on each one. Want some help with this, let's chat (learn more in the resource section). I have programs and services tailored to where you are on your ambitious path.

GATHER YOUR OWN DATA

If it's not clear by now, I love evidence as much as I love models and frameworks. As you're growing your business, having good data is important. I don't mean good data in the "I need to slap on a lab coat kind of way." I mean good *entrepreneurial* data. Information about you and your business that you can trust and that will help you make good decisions. We easily fall in love with our own ideas, programs, and services. We provide services because they bring us joy, which is awesome, but do they also bring us money? Because, ambitious one, that's important, too.

Striving for continuous improvement means ongoing reflection on what we've been doing— what's working well, what sucked, what projects or offers made us money, and which ones didn't. And we really can't rely on our memory for accurate information!

Entrepreneurial planning is most effective when based on real data that will help you see your business (and your life) in a different light. There's a chance you're flipping through this book, being irritated at my positive attitude, thinking, who is this person? I don't have time for self-care. I'm so busy, I hardly have time to breathe or do laundry, let alone go for a walk in nature. If this sounds like you, I encourage you to track your time for two weeks.

In 2012, I read *168 hours: You Have More Time Than You Think* by Laura Vanderkam. I was still at Women's Network. I was busy—managing complex projects, ferrying my kids to school, daycare, and sports, supporting my dad when he needed it, and commuting 1.5 hours each day.

I took Vanderkam's advice and tracked my time for two weeks, and a few interesting things emerged: I believed I worked 60 hours a week when, in fact, I worked 48. Still a lot, but a whole 12 hours less per week than I thought. I spent more time on social media than I imagined, and seeing 7.5 hours each week dedicated to driving back and forth to work was a wake-up call.

I took action on the commute time and started working at home a day or two a week—I treated those 90 minutes each day as free. I could work a little more or get supper ready (I didn't have the self-care dialled in at that point).

Take the next two weeks and track your time. I promise you'll discover aspects of your life that you overestimate and others that you underestimate (cough: social media), and if I'm wrong, send me a note. I'll buy you a coffee (and ask you to share your mad skillz).

Your tracking doesn't have to be perfect, but it should give you the broad strokes of day. Jot down in a notebook how often you "hop onto social media for a few minutes" and add them up at the end of the day, if tracking each time feels like too much for you.

I promise you have time to build in a little "you" time. Start small—address the low-hanging fruit, like I did with my commute time. It may be the fifteen minutes before your kids get going in the morning or the fifteen minutes before bed, but it's there, and tiny steps build momentum.

BE WILLING TO MAKE STRUCTURAL CHANGES

Putting yourself first and practicing first aid means you will probably want to make some changes. I was talking to my friend and fellow business owner Hélène after she'd been "sheltering in place" with her family for months and months as a result of COVID-19 public health measures.

When she did her business year in review, she realized that she lost a lot of time and had a lot of interruptions in her day from her family coming in and out of her office. They're not toddlers (who can be forgiven for such things). They're teenagers and young adults who were interrupting for a perfectly reasonable reason—they needed to grab a document off the printer. Totally fair, but still distracting and impacting her productivity and bottom line, so the solution? They moved the printer. A very simple structural change allowed her to have more focus and fewer interruptions.

Recently, a client wanted to break her micro-manager habit. Through our session, she made a structural shift that addressed both issues: Rather than mapping out the project/work plan for her team in their software, she created a template and empowered them to do it. Bam. Simple structural shift—more time, less micromanaging.

Be on the lookout for the structural changes that you can implement to make your day's work better for you.

LEARN THE *SAA TAA NAA MAA* EXERCISE

A few years ago, I was presenting a time management workshop to tourism operators attending a day-long workshop. I was also supporting a friend through a difficult situation in her workplace and our community. I was raging against the patriarchy, hating the silencing, disbelieving, judging, and oppression that women often face when they speak their truth. While I did the presentation, I struggled to stay present with these issues rattling around in my brain and my emotions running high.

I wanted nothing more than to dash out of that room as fast as I could, but I felt compelled to stay until the break, where my exit would be less noticeable. A local yoga instructor, Erica Killam, was up next. She taught the group chair yoga, as I watched the clock, my mind spinning wildly.

But then she shifted to guided meditation. She told everyone to sit quietly in our chairs with our eyes closed and to tap our fingers on our thumbs, while saying, *"saa taa naa maa,"* which loosely translated from Sanskrit, means, "this too shall pass." We did this for six minutes, tapping, *Saa* (baby finger to thumb), *Taa,* (ring finger to thumb), *Naa* (middle finger to thumb), *Maa* (pointer finger to thumb). This too shall pass.

Woah. It was one of the more profound experiences I've had in my life.

Especially remarkable given I was in an industry association annual general meeting full of people I didn't know and only was still there because I didn't want to be disruptive to the next presenter. I went from being ramped up, raging, furious over my lack of control or ability to influence or change this circumstance to relaxed . . . chill . . . and with a deepened awareness that this too shall pass. That nothing—good or bad—lasts forever. Nothing is permanent.

I wandered around the whole weekend tapping my fingers, and I continue to use this meditation when I'm feeling like I need a reminder of life's impermanence.

Saa taa naa maa. This too shall pass. Sometimes, like my favourite COVID meme says, it may pass like a kidney stone, but it will pass. This too shall pass. *Saa taa naa maa.*

ONE CHANGE = MANY GAINS

A few years ago, when I was getting to the end of a long phase of dizziness, I was feeling increasingly anxious about leaving the house, but I still needed to make the 45-minute drive to Charlottetown to meet with clients.

My super sweet husband assured me that he would come and pick me up anytime I needed him to. And in a two-week period in December 2018, he picked me up three times. It was awful, being stuck and dizzy and sick, but knowing that he was chill and willing to help reduced my anxiety and helped me maintain a (slightly) better attitude.

I was trying to keep things light and see the positive. Yet, while Scott was willing to rescue me when I needed it, he's not always available, and it's still stressful feeling stranded. So, I made a tactical change that helped everyone.

Just before the COVID shutdown in March 2020, I rented a tiny studio apartment/office in Charlottetown, which I share with a friend. Now when I'm feeling episodic, it brings me comfort to know that I have a place to rest and recover if I need it. Having that space allows me to do the things I need to do to maintain optimum health and be my ambitious self.

CONTINUE...

STORY TIME CONTINUED...

Now, if I have a morning meeting, I stay at the tiny apartment overnight, which allows me to maintain my morning routine and reduce the franticness, which I don't handle well anymore. It also cuts down on travel time when I have business in the city, giving me more time to work on revenue-producing activities.

I'm aware of the massive privilege I have in this story: a supportive partner, a car to myself, and enough resources to have an apartment/office away from home. It wasn't an easy yes for me to take the apartment in town. Sharing it makes the rent reasonable, but I worried that people would judge me. But it makes so much sense for me. I hope that you're inspired to find creative ways to make your life work better for you, depending on the resources that you have available.

SHE RULE FOUR: ATTITUDE IS EVERYTHING

"Life is 10% what happens to me and 90% of how I react to it. And so it is with you . . . we are in charge of our attitudes." – Charles R. Swindoll

Objectively, the long-term outcome for someone who has Meniere's Disease can be pretty terrible. There's no known cause, there's no known cure. And because it's rare, there's not much research or understanding of it either. There's a possibility that the symptoms will disappear, but only when the disease causes complete deafness in my left ear. From a medical perspective, this is considered one of the best scenarios.

There's also the potential that the dizziness and tinnitus (ringing in the ears) will become completely disabling. If it gets to this stage, the treatments are horrible, ranging from steroid shots in the ears to severing the vestibular nerve between the two ears, essentially interrupting the balance system in your body. It's really not fun. I find it hard to even write that shit down.

I could live in a world where I worry about Meniere's Disease all the time, when I'm having dizzy days and when I'm having long periods of wellness (wondering when will the good days end). I could be consumed by this stupid illness. But I choose not to be. Instead, I choose Magical Thinking: The belief that my thoughts, wishes, and desires can influence my external world.

I literally wear rose-coloured glasses for no other reason than my daily reminder to look on the bright side. They make the world look brighter on cloudy days. Our beautiful PEI sunsets are more magnificent, and rainbows look a little more enchanting.

I choose to be positive. I choose to be optimistic. I choose to see the good things in life. I choose to run the risk of people seeing me as a Pollyanna— or worse, inflicting toxic positivity on them. Because I firmly believe that where I focus my thoughts, my time, and my energy does influence my external world.

And it is not always easy on the days when I struggle to get out of bed because I'm dizzy. Or on the days when my plans are derailed by a dizzy spell. Or when I'm bone-tired after months and months of ongoing sickness. Or on the days when I feel anxious about leaving the house for fear of getting dizzy without the comfort of my bed close by. Or when I'm feeling depressed and my mind wanders to a Meniere's-fuelled terrible future.

And yet, I know that even in those difficult times, as long as I focus my energy and attention on the good things that are happening in my life, I feel better. Not "my life is 100% amazing" better, but I can generally find the next-best-feeling place if I look for it. I can usually find the beauty in the day if I look for it. But let's be clear: sometimes I have to dig deep.

I move myself from:

"I'm a terrible mother—I can't even get out of bed to feed the kids" to "I'm grateful my kids are old enough to fend for themselves, even if it's boxed pizza and Mr. Noodles."

from:

"What an awful coach I am, having to cancel today's session" to "X client will be a-okay having an unexpected free hour in their day."

from:

"My life sucks so hard" to "Things have been this bad before, and I'll have periods of wellness again."

I was surprised, when I was doing the research for this book, that Magical Thinking is described derisively, a foolish phenomenon commonly seen in young children before they come to know better. I actually love the idea of

Magical Thinking—who doesn't want a little magic in their lives?

But perhaps it's more helpful to frame it as positive thinking. According to wellness mentor Lisa Woods (2019), "Positive thinking encompasses the mental attitude of optimism, which searches for favorable outcomes in all situations. It relies on the emotional state of hope, which looks past the current circumstance and supports the building of emotional, social, and other resources for positive action." Positive thinkers make the best out of every situation, focusing on what they can control, letting go of what they cannot, and searching for ways to improve the situation, while being mindful of any lessons to learn.

Having a positive mental attitude (and believing in a little magic) helps with your emotional resilience through the storms. Like the quote says, life comes down to choices. You chose to rely on your partner, which not everyone would do. You also chose to sacrifice some income in order to save time. You can choose to be vulnerable rather than pretending to be invincible.

It all circles back to attitude. We get to decide our attitude toward our experiences and our circumstances. I believe that the Universe is helping us out. The more I focus on my core values, do things that are in alignment with those values, keep a good attitude, and remember what's important to me, the more the Universe seems to deliver. Maybe it's magic. Maybe it's positivity coming back to me. Maybe it's the momentum I'm building. Maybe my team is getting better at writing sales and marketing copy. Whatever it is, it works.

I know that for lots of us, it's really hard to have a positive attitude in the face of relentless shitty circumstances and situations. It takes a lot of effort to remember and refocus, but with time and tiny steps, it does get easier.

The following pages provide some practical guidance on how to apply this

She Rule and have a positive attitude toward things, even when you're not feeling it.

Remember you can download the bonus She Rules Workbook at
https://sherules.biz/workbook.

HOW TO STAY POSITIVE

KNOW THERE'S NO ELEGANT SOLUTION

Behind the scenes, businesses are messy. We look at our mess and imagine the seamless behind-the-scenes of other businesses, so we go looking for elegant solutions to our problems. What I can tell you from looking under the hood of many businesses is that they are all messy! It never really looks as good as it does on social media or your sales page.

Release yourself from the need for perfectionism—done is better than perfect. There are no all-in-one solutions. And you will have tools, systems, and processes that will adapt as you need over time. Rest assured, once you solve problems in one aspect of your business, you simply move on to the next area! And you will feel better when you release yourself from comparisons.

AVOID TOXIC PEOPLE

Negativity is draining, so I do my best to surround myself with positive energy. But what happens if you can't escape from the toxic folks? Let's first challenge your assumption that they must be in your life.

There is no need to have toxic friendships or employees, even if they've been around for a long time. In these situations, you get to choose. It might be painful to cut those ties, and you may have lingering heartache, but you won't regret it.

Admittedly, this strategy can be more challenging with family members. Some of our most difficult relationships are with family members. Old patterns. Intergenerational trauma. People can love you and be toxic at the same time. Do your best to make generous assumptions (skip ahead to the next She Rule) because they are likely dealing with their own stress and trauma.

If we choose to include toxic folks in our life, we need a game plan. Plan for those known unknowns that I wrote about in *She Rule 3*. Play around with options that work best for your situation. Limit interactions. Practise your segues from a convo you don't want to have to one that is slightly less negative. Pre-plan conversation topics that are lighthearted, practise boundary setting, and tell them you'd prefer to change topics. You know what might come up and sometimes the best thing you can do is have a plan.

I want to be clear, too, that there can be a blurry line between toxic and abusive. Should you decide a toxic relationship is in fact abusive (and you absolutely have the right to make that call), you don't have to continue that relationship. Even if it is with your mother or father. Aunt or uncle. Sibling or cousin.

MAKE THE DECISION OVER AND OVER

In a world of negative headlines and toxic energy, it's easy to get ground down. It's easy to become bone-tired. Sometimes, you just have to make the decision over and over and over again to get out of bed and be your ambitious self. To keep moving forward. To grow that business of yours and defy expectations and odds and societal norms while crushing the patriarchy.

This is how we do it, by the way. We crush the oppressive systems by getting back up. By doing the thing over and over. By making the same decision again and again. You decide that you'll keep moving forward, that you're going to be ambitious, and that you're going to grow your business. And it gets easier.

I think of the Japanese proverb, *Nana korobi ya oki,* which loosely translates to "fall down seven times and get up eight." Standing up after you fall is how you build resilience, a trait every entrepreneur needs. This works in business or in life.

People occasionally ask me how I lost so much weight. And the answer is simple. I chose to live a healthier lifestyle. Over and over and over and over and over and over again. I decided in 2017 to change my eating habits. Not an easy feat when I've had a long and unhealthy relationship with food. And I haven't been successful because I made one magical decision and then never overindulged again. Nope. I've had a lot of bumps along the way—some of which lasted for months. I've made and remade decisions around food hundreds and hundreds of times over the past four years.

Regardless of what you commit to—scaling your business, living a healthier lifestyle, creating content for social media, etc.—your enthusiasm will ebb and flow. Rather than beating yourself up when this happens, take the opportunity to be kind to yourself and simply recommit to your goal.

BE OKAY WITH BEING A PARADOX

Many things sucked in 2020. And yet lots of good things happened, too. I spent a lot of time asking people about their COVID silver lining in the summer and fall of 2020. I like that descriptor because it acknowledges the clouds—the giant, wildly terrible dark clouds of 2020—and yet allows us to acknowledge that there are positive things that have come out of it. There were so many COVID silver linings. COVID is a great paradox.

Rather than think in either/or language, I invite you to adopt yes/and, as in . . .

. . . *Yes,* COVID was awful, *and* I spent more time with my family.

. . . *Yes,* you can be a serious business owner *and* cancel a meeting.

. . . *Yes,* you can be fiercely ambitious *and* feel exhausted.

This is all okay. Embrace the whole of you who are. As my dear friend Maureen says, "no one is one-dimensional." Embrace all your dimensions.

EMBRACE THE 7% ZONE

When we live by the *She Rules*, we are redefining the military-inspired rules of business and playing outside society's rules for us. We are changing the system to work better for us and our sisters. We are building our business and creating wealth. So, naturally, we live outside our comfort zone. Where we stretch and grow. Where we learn how tough we are. How confident we can become.

I heard recently that maximum growth occurs when you live 7% outside your comfort zone. Phew, 7% seems so reasonable and achievable and not all that scary. It feels like you can easily jump back into your comfort zone if you need to for a bit.

Successful entrepreneurs, though, make a point to be outside their comfort zone regularly. In my Breakthrough interview with Julia Campbell, of JEMS Boutique & the Anne Store here on PEI, she told me that she makes it a goal to be uncomfortable every day. That being uncomfortable is a key part of her 7-figure stretching.

Whether it is turning her phone off for a few hours to play with her kids even when she knows there are important emails coming through. Or taking the leap and launching her own clothing line, or spending time in the Canton Fair in China choosing fabric, even though it's one of the most overwhelming places she's ever been.

Spending time outside your comfort zone is where growth happens in big and little ways. What are you going to do today that is 7% outside your comfort zone?

REMEMBER: YOU'VE DONE HARD THINGS BEFORE

When I'm feeling really miserable and unable to get out of bed, it's hard to focus on what I want. It's much easier to focus on what I don't want, which does nothing but fuel the fire of my misery. A game I play with myself is thinking about other times where I've done hard things. I remind myself that I've ridden this particular wave of illness before, and I survived the extraordinary pain of losing my dad. I've lived through all kinds of tough situations in my relationships, my work, and my life.

I remember what has helped me: I remind myself that time passes (saa taa

naa maa - See Learn the Saa Taa Naa Maa exercise in She Rule 4), the acute will not always be acute, and that being in nature has healing power.

If you're reading this and you're playing hurt, take a few minutes to remember those times when you've experienced hardship. Not to add this one to your compendium of hard times, but to remind yourself of what you did to overcome or get through them. That you are stronger than you think.

WHY ATTITUDE IS THE MOST IMPORTANT AND ANNOYING SHE RULE

In 2010, I created and delivered a career exploration program for vulnerable women. The early years of this program were focused on supporting women who had "multiple barriers to employment," many of whom were accessing social assistance for their basic needs. Some of the women we were working with were recovering from addictions, had mental illness or precarious mental health, and many of them were living in poverty. Oftentimes, these hardships were a result of the multiple traumas they had experienced. In short, these were women who had very difficult lives and wanted to make changes for themselves and their kids.

We did a powerful activity with the women called ROPES: Rite of Passage Experience. Over the course of a week, we participated in experience-based personal growth and development activities, including a ROPES course with a high ropes element. High ropes courses and climbing programs generally focus on personal achievements and ask participants to confront their personal fears and anxieties, with the intended outcome being an increase in confidence, positive risk-taking, and self-esteem.

CONTINUE...

STORY TIME CONTINUED...

Basically, the goal is to create a belief that if you can climb a tree and shimmy across a cable thirty feet in the air, you can do anything that life throws at you. And it's very effective!

The ROPES/personal development week was facilitated by five women, including Clara Roche. The participants loved Clara. She was well into her seventies at this point with a face full of wrinkles. She was deeply spiritual and religious, but not in an in-your-face kind of way. She loved to smoke cigarettes and prided herself on her hour-long walk each morning, no matter the weather. Although long retired from a career of public service, she was deeply committed to supporting the most vulnerable women in our community to find their voice, to make different choices despite their difficult circumstances, and, most importantly, to choose their attitudes.

At one point during the week, she shared the quote at the beginning of this chapter ("Life is 10% what happens to me and 90% of how I react to it. And so it is with you. . . we are in charge of our attitudes"), and it had a profound impact on me. I saw the impact it had on some of the women as well—how they began to move toward what they wanted. It comes from the following passage:

> *The longer I live, the more I realize the impact of attitude on life. Attitude, to me, is more important than facts. It is more important than the past, than education, than money, than circumstances, than failures, than successes, than what other people think or say or do. It is more*

CONTINUE...

STORY TIME CONTINUED...

important than appearance, giftedness or skill. It will make or break a company. . . . a church. . . .a home. The remarkable thing is we have a choice every day regarding the attitude we will embrace for that day. We cannot change our past. . . we cannot change the fact that people will act in a certain way. We cannot change the inevitable. The only thing we can do is play on the one string we have, and that is our attitude. . . I'm convinced that life is 10% what happens to me and 90% how I react to it. And so it is with you. . . we are in charge of our attitudes. (Charles Swindoll)

This idea that life is 10% what happens to us and 90% our attitude toward it is a cornerstone of *She Rules*. This is the most important rule for an ambitious woman (especially if you're playing hurt). And depending on your attitude, it can also be the most annoying. Because it puts the responsibility back on you.

And yet, where else would the responsibility lie? If your answer is a capitalist and colonial system that perpetuates oppression, racism, and sexism, that is a fair response. I recommend you read Rachel Rodgers' book *We All Should be Millionaires*. As a successful Black woman with a 7-figure plus business, she argues that no matter your background, no matter what systemic injustices are stacked against you, you can make more money. She makes a great argument, so go read it and then come on back, okay? In fact, I suggest you read *We Should All Be Millionaires* no matter who you are or where you are on your entrepreneurial journey.

SHE RULE FIVE: MAKE GENEROUS ASSUMPTIONS

If you're flipping through this book and haven't gone over She Rule Four just yet, you might want to circle back because this rule builds on Attitude is Everything. Essentially, making generous assumptions is a positive way to say, "Stop judging the heck out of yourself and others."

Making assumptions is often framed as a negative thing, and we're told not to do that. However, we actually make assumptions all the time—everything is just a story we are telling ourselves. Yes, we can gather facts, rather than assumptions, but it's a lot of work. It's much easier to just make generous assumptions.

A number of years ago, I had the opportunity to interview a woman who was a senior vice president of a multinational computer company in the 1980s. She was a trailblazer for women in corporate leadership. The research tells us that women in leadership positions often like to be the only women in the room. That they tend to pull the ladder up behind them. They believe if "I figured it out myself, other women should have to as well."

I was excited, nervous, and curious to have the opportunity to ask this woman her perspective on these issues. As I asked her about these things in relation to her own experience, it led to a great conversation.

She told me that as the only woman in senior management, she was aware of her own social capital on that team. She couldn't just bring issues related to women to the table because she would be judged for that. She said her focus needed to be doing her job, not advocating for the rights of women in the company and beyond. She was always willing to have coffee, to talk to women who were climbing the corporate ladder and help them along, but she rarely brought "women's issues" to the corporate boardroom.

It was so fascinating to hear her perspective. It is easy from our 21st century perspective to judge our trailblazing foremothers of the 1980s without understanding the context in which they were living and the challenges they faced that are unimaginable to us now.

While this woman may not have brought women's issues to the boardroom on the regular, she has spent decades since actively working to ensure the tech space includes more women. She uses her privilege, her voice, and her experience to advocate for women, focusing heavily on the investment community where women are still woefully underrepresented. She promotes careers in tech with kids, always with a focus on being inclusive. She's an angel investor and actively recruits others to invest in early-stage businesses as well.

The full dimensions of who she is become lost when we write her off as one of those corporate women who didn't support other women. When we make assumptions, we miss how she's translated her experience as an early leader in the tech industry into a retirement full of dedicated and impactful volunteer work.

This particular She Rule is about reserving judgement and being kind because everyone is living a life you know nothing about. Whether it's a powerhouse corporate woman of the 1980s or a frazzled server at the end of a long shift, they are doing the best they can in the moment they are in, with the tools they have. Try to recognize that people's lives are complicated and that nobody gets up in the morning and decides that today's the day I'm going to fuck everything up.

Making generous assumptions means giving people grace. It means showing kindness and extending goodwill. It means assuming people's intentions are positive even if we don't see that in their actions.

Look, I get it. We judge people all the time. Why do we do that? Well, it's probably a good time for a reminder: The patriarchy is sneaky. We judge others because we are taught to. "Internalized oppression" can be defined as the tendency of some women to regularly put down, make disparaging remarks about, and/or sabotage their own or other women's and girls' identity, potential, and success (Ni, 2020).

We are taught to look at ourselves through men's eyes, which means we look at ourselves and each other with sexist attitudes (or racist, homophobic, ableist, the list goes on). And we have a long history of enforcing rules and norms that don't serve us.

In other words, we judge ourselves and others based on unattainable beauty standards. We gossip about each other far more harshly than men. We perpetuate the stereotypes of what a good mother does and doesn't do. We assume women want to be mothers and are kinda judgy when they tell us they don't. We laugh at terrible women drivers. We slut-shame. The oppressed become the oppressor.

It's really quite boring.

Because we end up with a lot less time to own our power, to find our voice, to live in our zone of genius, to do the things we love, and to create the products that make our lives and the world a better place. This patriarchal system keeps us just where it wants us—voiceless, in our small box, doing the unpaid labour of the world, amusing ourselves by policing each other's parenting skills and pencil skirts.

These days, my clients tend to tell me I'm the least judgemental person they know. It's a huge compliment because I've been actively practicing this rule for many years. Working with vulnerable women who were complex and wonderful gave me lots of opportunities to learn and unlearn internalized attitudes about them . . . and, in turn, about myself as well.

Time and again, I've had real conversations with women who defied my assumptions about them . . .

- The politician who comes across as a hardass but is secretly convinced everyone is going to find out she's a fraud and that she doesn't know what she's doing . . .

- The woman who is rough around the edges. She looks like she's had a hard life, swears like a sailor, lives in poverty, yet ensures her kids have a hot breakfast in the morning so their brain can work well, even if it means she doesn't eat . . .

- The university student with straight A's, a gorgeous boyfriend, a new car, and a dangerously unhealthy eating disorder . . .

I started making generous assumptions of people because hundreds of conversations reminded me that we are complicated and complex human beings.

Don't get me wrong; it is easy to slip into judgement. I'm skilled at being generous, and I'm still judgy at times. And, by the way, judging people for being judgemental is still being judgemental. Sigh. I struggle with this one.

You'll feel so much better as you move along your path of making generous assumptions. Business moves at the speed of relationships, as does life. As you focus on ambitious growth and making ambitious changes in the world, having good relationships is important. One of the many lessons to come from the COVID-19 pandemic is how important human contact is for all of us. And making the assumption that everyone is doing the best that they can at the moment that they are in is a key to developing and strengthening those relationships. You will have more trust with those around you, which leads to better relationships.

This is also not nearly as altruistic as it might sound. Sometimes you will need/want/hope to receive grace from others. Like you, I'm a high performer, and I have high standards. And while I limit the impact Meniere's Disease has on my clients' lives, there are times when I need to reschedule. And so, I ask for grace and generally receive it. You can, too.

But here's the thing: We can't be generous with others if we're not being generous with ourselves. Remember: You're also doing the best you can. This is where we often fall down. We judge ourselves more harshly than we do others.

For example, I am very generous with others, but when my Meniere's Disease flared up around 2013, I had some serious internalized ableism going on. I had a deep, deep shame about my illness and about living with the unpredictability of a disability. I was convinced that if people knew, they wouldn't respect me. That we wouldn't get funding if they knew the leader wasn't always well. That my team seeing my vulnerability would negatively impact their impression of me as a leader. (I am aware now that none of this makes sense.)

I had all the time in the world for my clients and staff who had various health problems that occasionally impacted my life and our work together. However, I had no time for my disability. I held myself to a much higher standard than I would anyone else.

It was a lot to carry, and I'm glad I've lightened my load. The following pages are full of my favourite pearls of wisdom I've gleaned along the way. It will help you to make generous assumptions about others, but more importantly, about yourself.

Remember you can download the bonus She Rules Workbook at https://sherules.biz/workbook.

— HOW TO MAKE GENEROUS ASSUMPTIONS —

BE A VULNERABLE LEADER

In her book, *Dare to Lead,* Dr. Brené Brown defines vulnerability as "uncertainty, risk and emotional exposure" (Brown, 2019).

This one is hard for me. When I first started in business, I had a year-long crisis of confidence. I had experienced a lot of success in my not-for-profit career, I was known as a leader and an expert, and my extroverted Leo self was omfortable in that role. When I went out on my own as a business owner at age 45, I lost a big part of my identity. I didn't know what I was doing. I was worried all the time. It was a weird and uncomfortable experience for me.

And yet, one of the ways I improved my business was being honest and open about my crisis of confidence. I was taking a business coaching certification program at the time with twenty-five coaches in the USA and Canada. I was a baby compared to most of them, who were already seasoned business owners. You know what happened every time I uncomfortably expressed vulnerability and talked about my fears and concerns? They responded. They offered up their sales training for free, brainstormed ways I could market myself, provided feedback on my content, and held me accountable to doing the things that scared me.

Why is it a challenge to be vulnerable in our leadership? This goes back to our militaristic "winner take all" business strategy. Historically, business leaders were strong, masculine, stoic, and wouldn't want you to see a crack in the armour. There was no room in leadership for emotions, vulnerability, or feeling exposed. If they didn't know how to move through the problem or challenge, they belted back a drink and hoped the answer would come.

Expressing emotion is a well-used gender stereotype for women. It's one of those stories that we've been told—being overly emotional is unattractive and unpleasant to be around. A fear of being seen as too emotional or overly sensitive keeps us silent. It stifles our power. It keeps us from finding our true passion. How many times have you literally chosen not to speak for fear your voice would crack and they would *know*?

And yet, we know, from our own experience, that expressing vulnerability and being honest with ourselves and others has massive benefits in life and business.

There is a growing body of research about vulnerability and leadership, led by Brené Brown, but certainly lots of other folks are discovering it as well.

I had a huge laugh when I read Chris Vos' book *Never Split the Difference: Negotiating as if Your Life Depended on It*. While unsurprisingly manipulative, the FBI teaches its hostage negotiators to think like women—to be collaborative, to listen with empathy, to ensure the other person feels heard, etc. The skills are framed as groundbreaking and a whole new world when, in fact, it's a fairly natural tendency for many of us. Leave it to the FBI to think they invented emotional intelligence.

But here's the thing: Business is emotional. There's no doubt that it's uncomfortable to be authentic and honest. And yet, we are really frigging good at it. And being comfortable with vulnerability and emotions is beneficial to you and your clients. Cause you know what's emotional? Talking to your accountant about your finances, sharing the core values that build your brand with your marketing agency, performance reviews with staff, sharing content with a copywriter, posting content to social media, working with clients . . .

Every aspect of business has an emotional component. So rather than shrinking away from your emotions, own the heck out of them. Own your ability to make people comfortable enough to share their own. Turn that stereotype on its head.

Reinventing the rules of business means making room for different kinds of leadership. And once you get over yourself (and start treating yourself more kindly), it is freeing.

I could barely breathe the first time I told a client that I have Meniere's Disease, and now I'm putting it in a book for the world to see. Who knew?

There's an unexpected joy that comes with being real, from being able to say things like, "You know what? Writing a book is terrifying, and I'm doing it anyway."

It is hard to put yourself out there. Especially, these days when the world seems especially angry and harsh and polarizing. Social media can be especially cruel. And I know that my white, middle-class privilege buffers me.

It's also hard for other people to put themselves out there. You can respectfully disagree with them. You can hold space for someone else. You can listen and be curious.

You can talk about your own experience, which makes it easier for them to open up and ask for help. I taught an entrepreneurship course this year to twenty-five people in the creative sector. I openly talked about the mistakes I've made in business and in life. It was easier for them to talk about their budgeting challenges when I'd already talked about mine.

As much as we hate to admit it … we're human. Being comfortable with our own and others' vulnerability helps with making generous assumptions. When I think about vulnerability in leadership, I always think of Brené Brown's famous Ted Talk: "The Power of Vulnerability" (Brown, 2010). I suggest checking it out.

PLAY THE "WHAT IF" GAME

Speaking of Brené Brown, she also has a Netflix show called *The Call to Courage*, where she talks about this idea of the stories we tell ourselves, and it resonated deeply with me (Brown, 2019). Essentially, we can make our heads spin by jumping to conclusions with hardly any details. If I find myself stressed or worried about something, I'll often stop and think, *what story are you telling yourself right now, Sara?* It is fascinating what comes up when you stop and ask yourself this question.

We make all kinds of wild assumptions with very few facts to back them up. About ourselves and about other people. Everything we tell ourselves is a story. We can tell ourselves stories that grow our confidence, expand our mindset, and flex our imagination and innovation muscles. Or we can tell ourselves stories that do nothing more than hold us back. Be careful which ones you let become feature films in your head.

The stories we tell ourselves are key factors in our ability to make generous assumptions about other people. A simple exercise to change your thinking is to play the "what if" game:

- What if my speech bombs?

- What if people zone out?

- What if people leave?

- What if I forget the words?

- What if I remember all the words?

- What if I remember all the words and people love what I have to say?

- What if an ideal client (or twelve) books a call with me?

- What if I can turn that speech into a speaking tour?

- What if I'm invited to speak on **insert your hero's** podcast?

When you start to spin about what you imagine someone is thinking, stop and play the what if game. Because you can imagine a great outcome as easily as you can imagine a terrible one. When you replace negative thoughts with positive ones, you will feel better, and you will more likely have a positive outcome (if for no other reason than you are looking for it).

BE CURIOUS (THAT'S HOW WE LEARN)

About twelve years ago, I was fortunate enough to participate in mediation training for service providers who worked with women experiencing violence. Over two years, we learned an array of skills I still use every day. I don't like conflict, and I've seen how hard it is to repair broken relationships. However, I discovered that you can use the same principles to prevent (not avoid) conflict. Good planning and solid communication are the core of conflict prevention. And curiosity helps prevent problems.

A principle of mediation is that when trust is lacking, we assume the other person's intent is negative. We make assumptions (in the stories we tell ourselves) all the time, so the antidote to making negative assumptions is to be curious. When we're curious, we can find out what someone's interests are. And when we know what their interests are, we can have amazing conversations, and we can be wildly collaborative.

Some questions you can use are:

- What concerns you about …?

- What are the core issues here?

- What are you hoping to accomplish?

- And how would that help you?

- What are we up against here?

When you're curious, people will tell you what's happening. Curiosity helps us understand what someone else's core needs are, and then we can brainstorm ways to ensure everyone's needs are being met.

Of course, you'll also want to be curious with yourself as well. When you're beating yourself up for one thing or another, be curious. Dig around a little to better understand why you're having a strong reaction to a person, a situation, or an event. Understand what your needs are and be prepared to include them in your plans. It will make a world of difference and is yet another way you are defying the patriarchal system.

REFRAME YOUR LACK OF CONFIDENCE

One of the things that I hear pretty consistently from women business owners is about their lack of confidence. If you're in this camp, you're in good company. The 2012 Global Report by Global Entrepreneurship Monitor reports that women-led enterprises are two-and-a-half times more likely than majority-male-owned business owners to say that confidence was a major obstacle for them in building their business (Xavier et al., 2013). *Shocking,* I know.

I hate the "lack of confidence" narrative. A lot. Like A LOT. Remember, the stories we tell ourselves are important—are we creating a positive environment to flourish or continuing to perpetuate our lack mindset?

Our society loves to reinforce the "women are not confident" story. I think about this a lot because the stories that we tell ourselves are really important. And if we continue to tell ourselves that we're not confident, then how do we build that confidence?

Our society is built on the backs of women's unpaid labour—physical and emotional. Women bear the lion's share of childcare and household responsibilities. We are the sandwich generation—taking care of our parents, aunties, and uncles as well. We keep track of birthdays, shoe sizes, and when the rug needs to be steam cleaned next. We try to buck a systematic bias against women, and yet, the continual reminding that we have no confidence helps keep the system in check.

The patriarchy keeps us down by getting us to do its work.

But, Sara, you're thinking, *regardless of whether or not I'm doing the work of the patriarchy, I don't feel confident.* I get it. It's not easy to buck the stereotypes and live confidently when we're taught not to. Confidence and imposter syndrome are issues for every woman I know, regardless of their income bracket. And the varying degrees simply depend on experience and how much work they've done to overcome society's narrative for their life. Flip to the bonus section at the end of the book for a confidence-building exercise.

DECIDE IF GOOD ENOUGH IS GOOD ENOUGH

One of the more unpleasant aspects of my old career was that the mistakes I made were often on the backs of the vulnerable women I worked with. There were situations I handled poorly more than a decade ago that I still think about. I was doing my best, but it most certainly wasn't good enough.

What about those times when your good enough doesn't measure up to your own standards? Or those of the law? Or your faith? Or your marital vows? Or standard business practices?

The wild year of 2020 exposed more inequality than many people imagined existed (except, of course, those experiencing the inequality). In terms of the pandemic, people who live in poverty, immigrants, and racialized people are more likely to contract COVID (and yet, we're still not doing a great job of tracking demographic information). The same folks were more at risk of losing their job, having their hours cut, or working in high-risk sectors like the health care and service industries.

In Canada, we've come face-to-face again with our racist genocidal treatment of Indigenous people with the discovery of unmarked mass graves on the grounds of an Indian Residential School throughout the country.

My beloved feminism is experiencing its own reckoning. I knew the history of feminism was troubled. While the Famous Five in Canada fought for women to be seen as people (and not property) under the law, they also used their power and influence to push for legislation that led to the sterilization of nearly 3,000 Canadians they deemed unfit to have children. Many of the victims were poor, disabled, mentally ill, and/or Indigenous.

In *White Feminism* by Koa Beck, she speaks to the women's movement prioritizing issues and experiences of white women. In the 1960s and 1970s, second-wave feminists silenced voices in the movement that weren't white and privileged. It's easy to focus on the wins and the forward movement, only reading the history as written by the "winners."

Unfortunately, these are not historic events. From my own experience, in 2014, a number of local women's organizations hosted a national conference called A Bold Vision. It was designed to celebrate women's leadership and imagine the future for our country as designed by 23 women leaders in our country (a play on the "23 fathers of confederation" who first created a vision for our country 150 years ago).

If you ask most of the women who attended, the conference was a great success, and they loved it. But the Indigenous women who participated as Visionaries experienced racism at our conference. I didn't expect it and handled it poorly.

Less than a decade later, I know that the conference was life-changing for some, and it caused harm to others.

I have not figured out how to reconcile the privileges I experience as a result of racism and colonialism. How to atone for the sins of my ancestors. And my own. But I will try.

For now, whether it's with these big issues or when I failed to send my payroll remittances to the government on time, I acknowledge when my best isn't good enough. I sit with that. I try not to rationalize my actions into a better light. I am, though, kind with myself.

I promise to do better, now that I know better. I educate myself. I reflect on what I've done and make plans to do things differently next time. I actively support organizations working to make our world a better place for everyone. I intentionally integrate diversity, equity, and inclusion guidelines into my business. I seek out a diversity of contractors and team members.

If you don't feel as though your best is good enough, then it's on you to change it.

The women I harmed in my career don't need my tears. The Canada Revenue Agency doesn't care that I forgot to pay my remittances.

For the big and the little, you take responsibility, make a plan to do better, and move on.

Now, what happens when it's someone else's best that isn't good enough? I often talk to women who have staff who are underperforming.

We circle back to being kind, gentle, and firm. It's important to have conversations with people to figure out why they're not performing, to be clear on the expectations, and make decisions according to what will keep us in alignment with our vision and values.

HOW I CHANGED MY OWN NARRATIVE

Many years ago, when I was making about $40,000 a year, I had One of my long-held self-judgements is around my uncomfortable relationship with details. I'm not a "details person." I find details annoying, confusing, hard to see, boring, and stressful. I also find them important and full of information that, when compiled, form patterns of information that I love and see easily.

Over time, my narrative has evolved from:

1990–2010 I'm bad at details (because I was/am).

2010–2012 I'm often foiled by details (because I was/still sometimes am). I once missed a flight because I had the wrong date in my calendar—it cost me a lot of money to overcome that missed detail, and I never told anyone because I was so ashamed.*

2012–2016 Details are stupid (because they were/are). They cost me money and made me feel bad about myself when I missed something simple. I was sick of my detail-related mistakes.

2016–2020 Details are hard to see (because they are). In the past few years, I've been trying to be easier on myself and find ways to adapt to this personality trait —hello, calendar invitations with embedded zoom links. My Calendly automatic scheduler is a

CONTINUE...

STORY TIME CONTINUED..

thing of dreams, especially since beginning to work across time zones (so hard and important!). Annotated agendas, team members, and project management training that force me to consider the details—all tools I rely on constantly.

2020–present Details are so important to me that they are managed by other people (because they are). While I've had help for a while, at the end of 2020, I hired an online business manager, Crystal Coleman. The Universe was being a great business partner the day our paths crossed. Crystal keeps me organized, manages the day-to-day, and compiles details into information we can analyze and use to inform how we will grow the business.

If Crystal misses something, I shrug it off as a human error. But when I was in charge of that particular aspect of my business, if I'd missed the same thing, I would be so hard on myself.

You hold yourself to a higher standard than you hold anyone else. You beat yourself up and talk to yourself in ways you would never talk to our friends and colleagues. And you'd be devastated to hear your children (or nieces) judging themselves with such harsh words.

So just stop it. Be generous with yourself. Start today. Catch yourself early. Talk to yourself like you do your dear friends.

This is another way we can chip away at the patriarchy.

By coming to terms with our own imperfection and getting help for things we need, we make space for our zone of genius, to focus on making the changes we want to see in the world. And we make space for others to shine when they're doing what they do best.

**Admittedly, missing the detail on the NYC trip was expensive; it also meant that I got bumped to first class. On my very first trip to New York City, I flew from Montreal to Toronto first class—champagne and orange juice, full breakfast with cutlery … I didn't even know these things existed. It was super fun!

SHE RULE SIX: SUPPORT OTHER WOMEN

The rule of supporting other women is so natural to me that it's like trying to describe how to breathe. I've always felt supported by other women and done my best to always be supportive. When I was a kid, Women's Network PEI, the organization I led many years later, used to host women's festivals. My mom would take me and my sister to these events. They always had a program for girls. I loved these events—a space just for girls, where the facilitators asked about our lives and our experiences. And listened intently to the answers. My voice was heard and valued, which was not always my experience as a child.

I was a smart, opinionated, and bold kid. These traits were not always admired by the grown-ups around me. But the ones who mattered fostered this in me—my Aunt Patri, who gave me her full attention always; my grandparents, who doted on me in their own ways; my parents, who encouraged me even when I was annoying, and they were tired. Even when I demanded answers to hard questions or when I dyed my hair multi-colours, long before it was fashionable, or when I would write fiery letters to the editor.

I grew up with one sister. When we got older, my sister's three girls spent every summer of their youth with me. I worked for a feminist organization. I lived in a bubble surrounded by supportive women who were all working to improve the lives of other women.

In 2015, I attended a breakfast meeting where four women shared their experiences in business and public service. They were funny, told stories of old-school sexism at work, and how they managed it. They were so inspiring, and I hung on their every word. During the Q&A, someone asked, "What do you do when you don't feel supported by other women?"

I have no idea how they responded because I was so blown away by the question. It never occurred to me that women didn't support each other. It was certainly not my experience (save for one mean girl in grade school who I ditched from my experience at the end of junior high).

For weeks, I asked everyone I knew if they felt supported by other women.

And I heard stories that broke my heart. I talked about this with my friends Dawn and Kerry Anne because I wanted to do something. We created Get Up & Go: Breakfast for Women Leaders because we wanted to establish an environment where women could support each other. Where women could network in a way that felt comfortable. Where we could celebrate each other's successes. Where supporting, inspiring, and motivating each other was baked into the event.

We ran our breakfast series for a number of years with a predictable formula: We gathered at 7:30 am, fed everyone a nice breakfast, and allowed time for people to chat with the other women at their table. Then, I would interview a woman leader in our community. We gave time for more table conversations, where everyone could reflect on what they heard—what resonated, what didn't, what they'd likely keep thinking about, etc.

We ended with celebrations; you could celebrate your achievement, another woman in the room, or a woman who wasn't there but had exciting news. We heard about promotions, businesses launched, babies born, marathons run … By 8:55 am, we wrapped up so everyone could head out into the day.

There is nothing like the energy in a room full of amazing women. I loved those breakfasts because I'm fascinated and inspired by women's stories. The extraordinary in the ordinary. Their ability to overcome adversity. Their ability to put one foot in front of the other. To do hard things.

And then to be willing to share with a group of friends, colleagues, and strangers who consistently listened with whole hearts? Truly amazing.

And you know what? It worked. This is but one event that ties together my local community of women who support each other because we created an environment for them to come together.

Regardless of their age or walk of life, if you invite women to a space where they feel authentically welcome, they bring the magic. The walls dissolve and make room for real conversations. We make deep and meaningful connections that we carry into our business and personal life.

We hear often that entrepreneurship is lonely. I entirely reject this message.

It can be lonely if you haven't found your community. So, keep looking because it truly doesn't have to be. Community can mean a lot of things—push yourself to attend your local chamber of commerce mixers or join the local business women's association.

There are amazing communities to be found online as well. You can start today by joining the She Rules Facebook Community! It may take some time, but it is worth it to keep trying different organizations and events until you find something that works for you. And if you happen to be an established member of a community, be on the lookout for the folks who might need a warm smile and an invitation to join your conversation.

Want more ways to support other women in your day-to-day? Keep reading.

Remember you can download the bonus She Rules Workbook at https://sherules.biz/workbook.

———— HOW TO SUPPORT OTHER WOMEN ————

BUY FROM WOMEN

The most powerful way to support other women is with your wallet.

As a result of our unpaid labour, we control 85% of all consumer spending. We also control 100% of the spending in our business. While we're working to shed some of our unpaid labour, let's leverage this bit for good.

Purposefully choose to purchase from other women. Purposefully support women who are 2SLGBTQ+ Black, Indigenous, and/or women of colour. Purposefully support small businesses. Purposefully support local artists.

REACH BACK

"When you've worked hard, and done well, and walked through that doorway of opportunity, do not slam it shut behind you. You reach back and give other folks the same chances that helped you succeed."—Michelle Obama (Glamour, 2017)

There are many, many ways that you can reach back. Mentor. Buy. Teach. Speak on a panel. Offer a kind word. Give encouragement.

LOOK AHEAD

Look to the women who are a little further on their path—the mentors, the people that you admire—and reach out to them. The further ahead you get as a woman in business, the less of you there are, and the lonelier it can get. That woman you deeply admire and think is amazing? Don't think for one second that she doesn't also have dark days and wouldn't benefit from hearing how much you admire her and have learned from her.

One of my Breakthrough podcast guests, Trivina Barber, CEO of Priority VA, collects these messages in a folder on her computer, entitled, "For When I Feel Like Shit" (Roach-Lewis, 2020). Your words matter. (P.S., you should totally create one of those files as well!)

AMPLIFY OTHER WOMEN'S VOICES

Women's voices are not heard as often around decision-making tables.

Research (and sometimes experience) tells us that when a woman has an idea or makes a suggestion, a man builds on it, and then it becomes the man's idea. The wise women in the White House during Obama's administration interrupted this pattern by purposely amplifying women's voices (Crockett, 2016).

They experienced how tough it was for women to exert influence during the president's first term, so they devised a strategy called "amplification" to hammer across one another's points during meetings. After one woman offered an idea, if it wasn't acknowledged, another woman would repeat it and give her colleague credit for suggesting it. It's simple and effective.

We can amplify other women in business, women in our community, and women in politics by sharing stories on social media, recommending books, and celebrating the success of women around us.

CHEERLEAD, CHEERLEAD, CHEERLEAD

We've all experienced imposter syndrome. We all have great days, and we all have hard days. It never hurts to tell someone they're doing a good job or to acknowledge when someone has done something big (or little) to support you

Take five minutes a few times a week and send a note (handwritten ones via snail mail are especially lovely) to a woman you think is doing a great job or who is doing something hard. I assure you, even if they never acknowledge it, you've made their day.

SUPPORT THE CHANGE YOU WISH TO SEE IN THE WORLD

It is our responsibility as business owners to support organisations who are working to make the world a better place. You get to choose your cause—are you supporting environmental causes, anti-racist work, organizations who help kids get a solid start in the world? Working in the not-for-profit sector is hard work and folks need our support. You can volunteer, sit on a board, donate your time and expertise, or give them money. All will be welcome!

And one of the great things about making more money is that you have more money to support people or causes that you believe in.

CULTIVATE STRONG RELATIONSHIPS

Many years ago, I heard the saying, "we have two ears and one mouth, so we should listen twice as much as we speak." It was a hard lesson for an extrovert and Leo to learn. I have realized over the years that an important part of cultivating deep and meaningful relationships is being generous, thoughtful . . . and a good listener.

It's easy to learn to ask good questions (go to the *Be Curious* exercise in Rule 5 as a starting point).

To have solid relationships means surrounding yourself with good people. Being generous and thoughtful starts with being a good listener. And actively listening is an important way to support other women. When you listen, you'll know how to support. Does she need a kind ear? Advice? A connection to someone in your network? If you're a good listener, you'll know the answer.

REMEMBER OUR GRANDMOTHERS

Years ago, I attended an International Women's Day event hosted by the PEI Advisory Council on the Status of Women. They asked people to reflect on women they most admire in their life.

Many talked about their grandmothers. The challenges they faced . . . the strength they had . . . And it reminded me of a story my Grandma Dixon recounted from *Women Who Run with the Wolves* by Clarissa Pinkola Estés after we'd had a particularly spirited conversation inspired by an intro women's studies class in university. We were talking about the impact of gender-specific toys on kids—dolls versus Lego sets kinda thing. She couldn't quite see my argument, but the next morning she shared this story.

There was a young woman speaking to a large crowd. At one point, she looked down and saw she was standing on her grandmother's shoulders. She held out her hand because she wanted her grandmother to see what she could see. The grandmother shook her head and said no, her job was to keep the foundation strong so the granddaughter could see further than she could.

I think of this often when I'm having hard days. I think of that grandma who raised five young kids on her own after her husband tragically drowned when she was 35. Of my Grandma Roach who had thirteen children and spent about a decade of her life pregnant. She was the town administrator for thirty years, and she could compute complex math in her head quicker than I could on the calculator, all while smoking a cigarette, baking bread, and washing dishes. She was smarter than every one of the men she supported as mayor.

I also think of our collective foremothers. The women who gave birth at home year after year. The women who bucked tradition and convention. The women who advocated for rights they didn't see in their lifetime. The women who lived with violence. The women who had no access to education. The women just kept going despite the heavy weight of the patriarchy on their shoulders.

So, if you didn't have the chance to meet your grandmothers (or you did, and they fit into the "toxic people to avoid" category), you can draw on the strength of all of our grandmothers.

I channel their strength on the days when I struggle to see my own.

I remember that I am standing on their shoulders and that I hope someday to be holding up other women so they can see further than me.

BE WILLING TO SPEND MONEY TO SOLVE PROBLEMS

The path to 7 figures (or whatever you decide is financial freedom) is much easier when you learn to spend money to solve problems. It gets really good when you support other women to grow their businesses and do the work they love.

The more you grow, the more options you'll have for problem solving.

When you're making less than $100,000/year, there is very little money to hire anyone else because you likely need as much of that $100,000 for you! Now let's look at what happens when your revenues are $500,000. You have more money to spend on having people help you out in your business.

Even in the early days, you can outsource. I hired a bookkeeper within the first couple of months of my business. In the beginning, it cost $100/month to have a bookkeeper manage it for me. Best money I ever spent.

When I was just over the $100,000/year mark in business, I hired my first Virtual Assistant. Again, sometimes it feels like we couldn't possibly afford someone, but when you break it down, you can see how it is doable.

My VA cost $25/hour. In the beginning, she worked about 10 hours a month with me. That meant a $250/month expense, *and* with the 10 hours in my month that were now freed up, I could easily earn far more than I paid out. She's since moved on, but I continue to grow my team and outsource as much as I can.

By investing in experts to help me in my business, I've been able to double my revenues each year. Yes, I've spent more money, *and* I've made more money, too.

Finally, whether you're hiring staff or contractors, pay a living wage. A (male) mentor in my early years bragged about his strategy to find contractors who were at an early stage—great at their craft but not confident in their pricing, so he could get their best work before they realized they were undercharging. Gross.

Remember, as feminist business strategists, we are growing businesses and changing the rules at the same time. We are valuing all people's work. Pay a living wage to your staff. Ensure you're engaging contractors at an appropriate rate. You can keep a close eye on your money and make decisions that value other people's time and expertise as well.

You want to grow, and in order for that to happen, you need help. Spend money to hire people to help you grow. You're not going to get to 7 figures by doing it all myself!

WHY WE NEED OUR BUSINESS WOMEN FRIENDS

Recently, I had to make a hard decision in my business. I had agreed to do community consultations that would inform a sexual violence strategy for the province in which I live.

One of the reasons I left my job in the not-for-profit sector was burnout, so when this project came along, I thought long and hard about whether I would do it and what emotional toll and impact it would have on me and my team.

We were two weeks into the planning phase when a few small things happened back-to-back, and I freaked out. There's no other way of saying it. I had a lightning bolt moment and realized I couldn't do this project.

I wanted to back out of the work. I felt I was making the right decision, and yet, I wasn't sure I could trust myself, given how triggered I was.

Luckily, I was able to phone a friend. In fact, I was able to phone several friends. Over the period of a couple of hours, I got wise counsel from women whose business and community sense I really trust. They all gave me interestingly similar,

CONTINUE...

STORY TIME CONTINUED..

yet different, advice. Then, I gave myself a chance to sleep on it.

That is the joy of supporting other women because when you need their support, they're right there, ready to help you out.

It is not an easy decision to back out of any work, let alone important work. But for my own mental wellness, I had to admit that I didn't have the capacity that I thought I did to support my team. And while I knew that I was making the right decision, it was sure helpful to bounce that off some friends.

Your business friends are so important. They're the ones who are going to support you, give you advice, and a kick in the butt when you need it. They'll help you out, and they'll send work your way. They'll refer you, and you'll do the same thing for them. Of course, your business friends don't have to be women, but I've found there's a shorthand with other women in business. Despite our differences, we have shared experiences, which I find helpful and comforting.

Stop talking about those who don't support you or your business. Find your community. Find the women who'll respond immediately to your SOS text because, in all likelihood, you've already done the same for them.

Intentionally building relationships with other women in business feels fantastic. It's heartwarming to know I'm not in it alone. I love contributing to other people's successes in small and big ways. And celebrating each other's wins creates an energy that keeps us in this beautiful state of expansion while reminding us that we are all capable of achieving successes beyond our wildest dreams.

PARTING WORDS

HERE'S THE THING...

I don't like rules. It was a struggle to name this book until I realized that the statement "I don't like rules" is a story I told myself. I do like rules. I just don't like rules that I think are stupid. Like business strategies that don't recognize the reality and complexity of women's experience or the requirement to register your car each year on your birthday (seriously, why is that a thing?).

But I actually like rules and constraints and structure.

- I especially like the She Rules—the ones I've honed to survive and thrive as an ambitious woman with bold goals in this world. Thanks to these rules . . .

- I'm in alignment with my big vision and my values, so I make decisions easily.

- My self-care practises keep improving.

- I'm fine with adapting and recalibrating when I need to for the greater good.

- I remain mindful of the fact that life is 10% what happens to me and 90% how I perceive it.

- I make generous assumptions about myself and others and that makes me happier and keeps my skin looking great (haha!)...

- And I support other women, which is at the core of everything I do.

So, where do you want to end up? Probably the same as me … somewhere further down the path. There's more money to make. More good to do in the world. More of the things that make you happy!

As you're reading this book, if you remember just one thing, let it be this: Little changes add up to big results.

You can have abundance in whatever you dream of—including a 7-figure business with a 40% profit margin—by incorporating little changes and big leaps while keeping your eye on the prize.

GENTLE PRESSURE, RELENTLESSLY APPLIED TO YOUR LIFE AND YOUR BUSINESS, WILL RESULT IN SUCCESS

You will uncover your ambition as you build more momentum. You will care less about the opinions of people who don't support you when you have a community of women who do. You will be so much happier when you take off the patriarchal lenses for longer periods of time.

We can be the change we want to see, and change starts from within.

Let's do what we can to add ourselves to the count of high-earning women. Those 2%ers need our help. They're lonely in their success. With our help, we can clear the path and maybe put up some signage so that more of us can find the way.

I said earlier that timing is to opportunity what location is to real estate.

Friends, we have timing on our side.

Look at what's happening as a result of the #MeToo and #TimesUp movements. Significant progress has been made in our society in less than a decade. Sure, there is a lot more work to do, but change happens when women remember there is more that unites us than divides us.

I am energized and excited by the recent news that Knix (period underwear for women) founder Joanna Griffiths raised $53 million dollars to fund her expansion while pregnant. And refused to work with any investors who questioned the impact her pregnancy would have on the business.

There's Gina Paige, CEO of African Ancestry, which helps people of African descent trace their ancestral roots back to a specific present-day African country and tribe or ethnic group.

And Monica Eaton Cardone, who is an expert in the payments and eCommerce fields and is paving a path for women in the tech sector.

And Jennifer Harper of Cheekbone Beauty, an Indigenous-owned and founded Canadian cosmetics company. They create high quality, cruelty-free beauty products and include giving back to the community as a key component of their business mission.

And Sherry Stewart Deutschmann, who has translated her massive business success into a new business she founded in 2019. BrainTrust is a company dedicated to helping women entrepreneurs grow their businesses to $1 Million in annual revenue . . . and beyond.

And Tammy Roach, who is the first woman to own a car dealership on PEI and one of only a few in the country. She's selling cars and paving a path for women in a traditionally male industry.

But also, the woman I spoke to recently who decided to quit her job so she could fully dedicate herself to her business. And all the women who are using entrepreneurship to chart a new path for themselves and their loved ones.

I look at Invest Ottawa, the lead economic development agency for knowledge-based industries in Canada's capital. They recognized that their tech sector (like all of them) is skewed male. Since 2018, they have been working intentionally to build more diversity, inclusion, and a sense of belonging to every aspect of the organization.

Their success has not been without its bumps and challenges, but even those they translated into more success. In 2021, they kicked off with the SheBoot pitch competition, with ten women founders vying for $200,000 in funding on our virtual stage.

They share their strategies, approach, and learnings with other regions to help them explore opportunities to build similar networks and initiatives. So much progress can be made when you harness the collaborative power, expertise, and resources of a committed community. It is truly a case study for creating a movement.

Everywhere I look, there are inspiring women in business. Women I interviewed for the Breakthrough radio, my clients, the people I follow on LinkedIn and Instagram. I'm so glad you're still with me on this journey. As you integrate the She Rules, the wins will start to stack up. You might not even notice it happening. But as you continue to live your life and run your business, the outcomes will follow. You will create a ripple. When we all do this, we create a wave. And that's how the world keeps changing.

ACKNOWLEDGEMENTS

In the writing of this book, I couldn't have done it without generous and thoughtful feedback from Susan Richards, Kerry Anne MacDougall, Dawn Wilson, Maureen Hanley, Belina Caissie, Michelle MacCallum, Crystal Coleman, and Hélène Scott.

I am grateful to—

Rory MacLeod for the helpful structural edit,
for the copywriting genius of Jaime Lee Mann,
for Dawn Wilson's patience and care with research,
for the careful and thoughtful copy-editing from
Christine Gordon Manley,
to Liz Bedell for your proofreading,
and to Lorie Miller Hansen and Andrea Cinnamond for the beautiful book design.

I've had great help with this, but any mistakes you find are all mine.

Thank you to my small but ambitious team: My Business Manager Crystal Coleman and assistants Bernie Dias and Ashely Belpasso. They were endlessly patient with me telling them "the book is almost done" and kept the work going when I was enjoying and agonizing over the writing process. I'd also like to thank Josie Baker, who worked with me as a consultant in the not-for-profit division of my business for nine months in 2020/2021. Our many conversations helped inform my writing.

I would not have been able to spend the time I needed working on this book without the love and support of my family. Many thanks and much love to my husband Scott, who supports me unconditionally in every aspect of life.

My in-laws Danny and Loretta, as well as Lynn and Dennis—so many hours spent driving our kids around. Thank you!

To my mom, Beverley Roach MacDonald and my stepfather Gerry. Again, so much driving and many sleepovers. But also, Mumma, for all the things. I would not have been able to do this without the strong foundation you and Dad created for Su and me. So much love.

To my oldest kid, Jenn, who has challenged my feminism, inspired interesting conversations about capitalism, and in many ways gave me permission to write about women's experiences, even though our understanding about gender is expanding all the time.

To my youngest, Nathan, who has been a great cheerleader, reminds me to have a positive attitude, and was always willing to immerse himself in video games to give me time to write.

To my cousin Ellen MacPhee, for your enthusiasm about the book and the inspiration that we can do hard things.

And to Shannon Keenan, for your unending support in this book project and life in general.

To my clients, the women I interviewed for Breakthrough, my many mentors, colleagues, and friends, in my not-for-profit and business communities. I hope you see yourself in this book because I've thought a lot about each of you as I've been writing. I've learned (and unlearned) so much from all of you. And I am blessed to have all of you in my life.

And finally, thank you to you for reading this book. I do hope that you will practise these rules, share this message, make lots of money, and help create a world that is more equitable and just.

BONUS EXERCISE: HOW TO HAVE THE BOOMING CONFIDENCE OF OPRAH

You may know the expression "carry yourself with the confidence of a mediocre white man." The language needs an update, but the message still stands. Many men have confidence that stems from their privilege and generations of successful role models lighting the way.

They are safe in the knowledge that whatever the task, they are the man for the job — literally. Even if they lack skills or experience that could attribute to their "I've got this" swagger.

It's easy to feel confident about achieving a goal when you've seen countless other people **who look like you** achieve similar success.

Women are catching up. But the patriarchy whispers that we are less capable. So we tell ourselves that we don't have enough confidence to be a success-ful leader. (And if you're non-white, non-cis, differently-abled, plus-sized, or living below the poverty line . . . there's an even higher chance you haven't gotten the message that, actually, you ARE capable of success, too.)

So what is the patriarchy, anyway? And what should be the model we strive for, if not the often unearned "confidence of an average white man"?

The patriarchy is a complex system of gender politics that enforces strict and outdated norms, rules on our behaviour, and the way we interact with one another based on our gender. The patriarchy hurts everyone by reinforcing the belief that only men are capable of leadership (among other privileges).

I want us to let go of patriarchal language and develop 7-Figure Confidence instead.

7-Figure Confidence has three main features:

- It comes from experience and hard work. Not privilege.

- It grows stronger by listening to your intuition. Listen to your spidey senses if something doesn't feel good.

- It is preserved in your zone of genius and your womanhood.

It's time for you to develop an intuitive sense that you're capable. Women spend too much time in our heads, reinforcing tired stories. This confidence exercise might not give you the same strut of a world-famous TV billionaire like Oprah, but it's a start.

1 *Reframe "I'm not confident" to "I'm having a crisis of confidence."*

When I started my own business, I went from being a confident leader in my community to someone who knew nothing about starting a business. My first year in business was a massive crisis of confidence. I went from being someone who knew what to do in complicated and complex work situations to someone who knew none of the answers. I was not confident in my business savvy. And yet, I didn't lose my confidence in answering questions about women's experience, writing funding proposals, managing budgets, advocating for women, etc.

We all have areas of confidence, and we all have areas where we want to grow and stretch. Reframing your lack of confidence as a crisis instead makes it lighter. A crisis of confidence indicates that you have confidence (unlike a lack of confidence which suggests you have none). Which means it is easier to move through. Your crisis of confidence may be acute now, but it's not absolute. This too shall pass.

2 *Relax into your expertise.*

Think about the areas of your life where you do feel confident. Your area of expertise in your business, your ability to whip up a meal made from nothing, or your skills as a soccer coach.

I spent a lot of time figuring out what I could lean on from my not-for-profit experience to grow a business. I didn't know how to sell anything, but what I came to realize was that growing a small not-for-profit from $200,000/year in revenues to $900,000 was pretty similar to growing a business. I knew a lot about operations, team building, PR, marketing, budgeting, collaboration, negotiation. The list goes on. It just took some time to figure out which skills I had that could transfer to this new endeavour.

3   *Trust in other people's confidence in you.*

When I was struggling so hard in the early days of my business, I leaned on my friends and colleagues who were entirely confident in my ability when I couldn't see it. My friend Kerry Anne helped me develop my brand strategy. She was confident in my brand and what I had to offer the world, so when I couldn't see it myself, I trusted her confidence in me.

4   *What other people think about you is none of your business.*

We can lose so much time worrying about what other people think of us. I get it. Trust me, I do. I live in a tiny place, where two degrees of separation is more common than six. We all worry about what people think about us. And the more successful you become, the more likely it is that people are going to have opinions about you. And, ideally, the more successful you become, the more focused you are on building your empire, supporting your clients, and loving your life, not on others' opinions. It stings, but it only hurts if you let it.

5   *Build your skills.*

One way to boost your confidence is to build your skills. I took a coaching certification program when I first started—it was super helpful to learn some new skills to build out another area of expertise for myself.

If you think about the areas where you are confident—where you have a great deal of expertise—they've likely been built by education and experience over time, whether that was in a formal setting or all of the things that you may have learned in your career. Build your knowledge.

I have a program called 7 Figure Confidence that does exactly this. It helps you figure out the business side of your business. You are the expert in your business, and I bring an expertise to how to plan and strategize and make your business work for you.

6 *Action is the only antidote to a lack of confidence.*

Imperfect action is the only antidote to a lack of confidence. The more you do, the better you get, and the only way you get better and more confident in any area is just to do it. I promise you, no one is looking at you as closely as you are.

A mentor said to me one time, if you're not a little bit embarrassed by the first offer you put out into the world, you waited too long. Stop being paralyzed by perfection. Done is better than perfect. You'll learn so much. And feel more and more confident as a result.

Ask yourself, what influence am I under right now? Is this patriarchal judgement at work? Or do I need to deepen my skills and knowledge to boost my confidence in a specific area? Do I need to change the stories I tell myself?

SUMMARY

Despite the stories you tell yourself or roles projected by a patriarchal society, you can buck the stereotypes and live confidently. It won't always be easy.

But a mindset switch can be just the thing to become a confident business owner and flourish.

RESOURCES

Here's a list of the books, programs, and other resources I've referenced in She Rules. These are tried and tested in my own life and ones I often recommend to clients. You can find more information or access any of these with a quick google search.

BOOKS:

Alinsky, Saul, (1971) Rules for Radicals

Beck, Koa (2021, January 5) White Feminism

Brown, B. (2019). Dare to Lead: Brave work, tough conversations, whole hearts. Random House Large Print Publishing

Clear, James. (2018) Atomic Habits

Duke, Annie. (2019). Thinking in Bets: Making smarter decisions when you don't have all the facts. Portfolio/Penguin

Hendricks, Gay. (2009) The Big Leap

Michalowicz, Mike (2020). Fix This Next

Michalowicz, Mike (2014). Profit-First

Rodgers, Rachel (2021). We Should All Be Millionaires

Rodsky, Eve (2021). Fair Play: A game-changing solution for when you have too much to do (and more life to live). G. P. Putnam's Sons

Tzu, Sun, (5th century BC, reprinted 2011). The Art of War

Vanderkam, Laura (2010) 168 Hours

Veloso, M. (2004). Web Copy That Sells: The revolutionary formula for creating killer copy every time. Amazon

Vos, Chris, (2016) Never Split the Difference: Negotiating as if your life depended on it

Williamson, Marianne, (1992). A Return to Love: Reflections on the principles of "A Course in Miracles"

PROGRAMS AND SERVICES:

7-Figure Confidence, Sara Roach Lewis

90 For 90 Challenge, Sara Roach Lewis

She Rules Facebook Group, https://www.sherules.biz/community

Create Your Online Course in 30 Days Flat, Heather Deveaux

Numbercrunch, Susan Richards

Invest Ottawa, International Women's Week Programming

Women's Network PEI

VIDEOS/PODCASTS/ARTICLES:

Breakthrough, with Sara Roach-Lewis. VoiceAmerica

Focus Forward Podcast for Business Owners

Kirtan Kriya - Sa Ta Na Ma, Meditation. YouTube

Power + Presence + Position, Eleanor Beaton

The Call to Courage, Brené Brown. Netflix

The Tim Ferriss Show (Podcast)

Todd Herman's Stages of Business Growth

REFERENCES:

Alinsky, S. D. (1971). Rules for Radicals: A practical primer for realistic radicals. Random House

Allen, C. (2018, December 11). The media and its promotion of negative body image. Medium. https://medium.com/@carrieallen341/the-media-and-its-promotion-of-negative-body-image-9ba7887de766

Beaton, E. (Host). (2021, June 15). How to avoid broke millionaire syndrome with Jackie Porter (No. 459) (Audio podcast episode). In Power + Presence + Position. Eleanor Beaton. https://eleanorbeaton.com/fierce-insights/ep459-how-to-avoid-broke-millionaire-syndrome

Beaton, E. (Host). (2017-present). Power + Presence + Position (Audio podcast). Eleanor Beaton. https://www.eleanorbeatonpodcast.com

Beck, K. (2021). White Feminism: From the suffragettes to influencers and who they leave behind. Atria Books, an imprint of Simon & Schuster, Inc.

Bittner, A., & Lau, B. (2021, February 25). Women-led startups received just 2.3% of VC funding in 2020. Harvard Business Review. https://hbr.org/2021/02/women-led-startups-received-just-2-3-of-vc-funding-in-2020

Bouchard, I., & Bédard-Maltais, P.-O. (2019). (rep.). The Changing Face of Canadian Entrepreneurship. BDC . Retrieved from https://www.bdc.ca/EN/Documents/analysis_research/bdc-etude-sbw-nation-entrepreneurs.pdf?utm_campaign=Changing-faces-Study-2019-EN

Brown, B. (2010, June). The Power of Vulnerability. TED. https://www.ted.com/talks/brene_brown_the_power_of_vulnerability?language=en

Brown, B. (2019). Dare to Lead: Brave work, tough conversations, whole hearts. Random House Large Print Publishing

Bundles, A. L. (2020). All About Madam C. J. Walker. https://madamcjwalker.com/about/

Brown, B. (2019, April 19). Brené Brown: The Call to Courage. Netflix Official Site. https://www.netflix.com/title/81010166

Canada, W. A. G. E. (2021, April 14). Government of Canada. Women and Gender Equality Canada. https://women-gender-equality.canada.ca/en/commemorations-celebrations/womens-history-month/persons-day.html

Canadian Women's Foundation. (2021, June 5). The Gender Pay Gap: Wage gap in Canada: The facts. Canadian Women's Foundation. http://canadianwomen.org/the-facts/the-gender-pay-gap

Cardone, G. (2011). The 10x Rule: The only difference between success and failure. John Wiley & Sons

Catalyst. (2020, March 13). Women on Corporate Boards (quick take). Catalyst. https://www.catalyst.org/research/women-on-corporate-boards/

Crockett, E. (2016, September 14). The amazing tool that women in the White House used to fight gender bias. Vox. https://www.vox.com/2016/9/14/12914370/white-house-obama-women-gender-bias-amplification

Devillard, S., Vogel, T., Pickersgill, A., Madgavkar, A., Nowski, T., Krishnan, M., Pan, T., & Kechrid, D. (2019). (rep.). The Power of Parity: Advancing women's equality in Canada. McKinsey & Company. Retrieved from https://www.mckinsey.com/featured-insights/gender-equality/the-power-of-parity-advancing-womens-equality-in-canada

Dotti Sani, G. M., & Treas, J. (2016). Educational gradients in parents' child-care time across countries, 1965-2012. Journal of Marriage and Family, 78(4), 1083–1096. https://doi.org/10.1111/jomf.12305

Duke, A. (2019). Thinking in Bets: Making smarter decisions when you don't have all the facts. Portfolio/Penguin

Estés, C. P. (1992). Women Who Run With the Wolves. Ballantine Books

Ferriss, T. (2021, July 26). Podcast - The Tim Ferriss Show. The Blog of Author Tim Ferriss. https://tim.blog/podcast/

FreshBooks. (n.d.). New research from FreshBooks discovers a 28% wage gap among self-employed women and men. FreshBooks. https://www.freshbooks.com/press/data-research/women-in-the-workforce-2018

Geena Davis Inclusion Quotient. (n.d.). (rep.). The Reel Truth: Women aren't seen or heard an automated analysis of gender representation in popular films. Retrieved from https://seejane.org/wp-content/uploads/gdiq-reel-truth-women-arent-seen-or-heard-automated-analysis.pdf

Glamour. (2017, January 1). 10 Michelle Obama Quotes We Need Now More Than Ever. Glamour. https://www.glamour.com/gallery/10-michelle-obama-quotes-we-need-now-more-than-ever

Global Media Monitoring Project. (2021). (rep.). Who Makes The News. The Global Media Monitoring Project. Retrieved from https://whomakesthenews.org/wp-content/uploads/2021/07/GMMP2020.ENG_.FINAL20210713.pdf

Government of Canada, S. C. (2021, April 26). Intimate partner violence in Canada, 2018. The Daily. https://www150.statcan.gc.ca/n1/daily-quotidien/210426/dq210426b-eng.html

Hayes, J., Hess, C., & Ahmed, T. (2020). (rep.). Providing Unpaid Household and Care Work in the United States: Uncovering inequality. Retrieved from https://iwpr.org/wp-content/uploads/2020/01/IWPR-Providing-Unpaid-Household-and-Care-Work-in-the-United-States-Uncovering-Inequality.pdf

Herman, T. (2019, August 15). The 5 Stages of Business Growth - 90 Day Year: A Peak Performance Approach to Business. https://www.90dayyear.com/the-five-stages-of-business/

Jackson, A. P. (2016, April 23). The Pitfalls of Gender Socialization for Women. Zanesville Times Recorder. https://www.zanesvilletimesrecorder.com/story/opinion/2016/04/23/pitfalls-gender-socialization-women/83240918/

Johnston, L. (1983). More Recollections Of An 'Ole Salt. Prince Edward Island Heritage

Klaff, O. (2011). Pitch Anything: An innovative method for presenting, persuading and winning the deal. McGraw-Hill

Mackelden, A. (2021, March 12). Lady Gaga discusses her "psychotic break" and chronic pain with Oprah. Harper's Bazarr. https://www.harpersbazaar.com/celebrity/latest/a30414700/lady-gaga-oprah-interview-psychotic-break-chronic-illness/

McNeilly, M. (2013, November 11). Fighting Your Business Battles: 6 lasting lessons from Sun Tzu's art of war. Fast Company. https://www.fastcompany.com/3021122/fighting-your-business-battles-6-lasting-lessons-from-sun-tzus-art-of-war

Ni, P. (2020, May 17). 10 Signs of Internalized Sexism and Gaslighting. Psychology Today. https://www.psychologytoday.com/ca/blog/communication-success/202005/10-signs-internalized-sexism-and-gaslighting

Public Service Alliance of Canada. (2019, March 6). Canadian Women's History. Public Service Alliance of Canada. https://psac-ncr.com canadian-womens-history

Roach-Lewis, S. (2020, March 4). E8: Trivinia Barber - Expert Advice on Outsourcing Outcomes and Risks. SRL Solutions. https://www.srl. solutions/trivinia-barber-expert-advice-on-outsourcing-outcomes-and-risks/

Rodgers, R. (2021). We Should All Be Millionaires: A woman's guide to earning more, building wealth, and gaining economic power. HarperCollins Leadership, an imprint of HarperCollins

Rodsky, E. (2021). Fair Play: A game-changing solution for when you have too much to do (and more life to live). G. P. Putnam's Sons

Shi, R., Kay, K., & Somani, R. (2019, March 8). Five facts about gender equality in the public sector. World Bank Blogs. https://blogs.worldbank. org/governance/five-facts-about-gender-equality-public-sector

Steinmetz, K. (2020, February 20). Kimberlé Crenshaw on what intersectionality means today. Time. https://time.com/5786710/kimberle-crenshaw-intersectionality/

Swindoll, C. R. (n.d.). Charles R. Swindoll Quotes (author of the Grace Awakening). Goodreads. https://www.goodreads.com/author/quotes/5139.Charles_R_Swindoll

Taylor, C. (2019, October 7). A third of the world's female entrepreneurs face gender bias from investors, HSBC claims. CNBC. https://www.cnbc. com/2019/10/03/hsbc-a-third-of-the-worlds-female-entrepreneurs-face-gender-bias.html

UN Women. (2021, January 15). Facts and Figures: Women's leadership and political participation: What we do. UN Women. https://www.unwomen. org/en/what-we-do/leadership-and-political-participation/facts-and-figures

Vanderkam, L. (2011). 168 Hours: You have more time than you think. Penguin

Vanderkam, L. (2020, March 30). Writer, Author & Speaker: Time management. https://lauravanderkam.com/

Vaynerchuk, G., Gary Vaynerchuk author's page https://www.garyvaynerchuk.com/books/

Veloso, M. (2004). Web Copy That Sells: The revolutionary formula for creating killer copy every time. Amazon

Voss, C., & Raz, T. (2017). Never Split the Difference: Negotiating as if your life depended on it. Random House

Whitford, E. (2020, April 15). Pay and seniority gaps persist for women and minority administrators in higher education. https://www.insidehighered.com/news/2020/04/15/pay-and-seniority-gaps-persist-women-and-minority-administrators-higher-education

Williamson, M. (2012). A Return to Love: Reflections on the principles of "A Course in Miracles". HarperOne

Women's Business Ownership Act of 1988, Pub. L. .No. 100-533, 102 Stat. 2689 (1988). https://www.govinfo.gov/content/pkg/Statute-102/pdf/Statute-102-Pg2689.pdf

Women Entrepreneurship Knowledge Hub. (2020). (rep.). The State of Women's Entrepreneurship in Canada 2020. Women Entrepreneurship Knowledge Hub. Retrieved from https://wekh.ca/research/the-state-of-womens-entrepreneurship-in-canada/

Woods, L. (2019, September 24). 3 Scientific studies that prove the power of positive thinking. Medium. https://medium.com/swlh/3-scientific-studies-that-prove-the-power-of-positive-thinking-616477838555

Xavier, S. R., Kelley, D., Kew, J., Herrington, M., & Vorderwülbecke, A. (2013). (rep.). Global Entrepreneurship Monitor: 2012 Global Report. Global Entrepreneurship Monitor. Retrieved from https://www.gemconsortium.org/report/gem-2012-global-report

WORK WITH SARA

COACHING

IF YOU ARE AN ambitious woman, Sara would love to hear from you about how she can help you scale your business.

SPEAKING

WANT TO FIRE UP an audience of entrepreneurial women? Sara is an experienced speaker with a message that will resonate long after your event ends.

TRAINING

SARA HAS HOSTED NUMEROUS programs and workshops focused on the unique needs of women in business.

For more information, visit **www.sherules.biz** or email **info@sherules.biz**

IF YOU ARE AN anxious woman,
Sara would love to hear from you
about how she can help you seek
your dreams.

WANT TO FIRE UP an audience of
entrepreneurial women? Sara is an
experienced speaker with a message
that will be with them long after your
event ends.

SARA HAS HOSTED NUMEROUS
programs and workshops centered
on the unique needs of women in
business.

For more information, visit www.sherules.biz
or email info@sherules.biz

—CONTINUE THE CONVERSATION—

JOIN US ON FACEBOOK

Connect with other ambitious women who are also applying the **She Rules** in **their business**

- COMMUNITY
- INSPIRATION
- ACTION

www.sherules.biz/community FB for **She Rules Biz**